Skills-based Caring for a Loved One with an Eating Disorder

Skills-based Caring equips carers with the skills and knowledge needed to support those suffering from an eating disorder, and to help them to break free from the traps that prevent recovery. Through a coordinated approach, it offers detailed techniques and strategies, which aim to improve professionals' and carers' ability to build continuity of support for their loved ones.

Using evidence-based research and personal experience, the authors advise the reader on a number of difficult areas in caring for someone with an eating disorder. This new and updated edition is essential reading for both professionals and families involved in the care and support of anyone with an eating disorder.

Professor Janet Treasure OBE, PhD, FRCP, FRCPsych is a psychiatrist who works in research and teaching at King's College London and as a clinician at the South London and Maudsley NHS Foundation Trust. Professor Treasure's research interests include conjoint working with patients and carers using translational research to develop new forms of treatment. From this she has coproduced a set of tools that provide shared information about the illness and skills in management.

Gráinne Smith, author and former teacher, has talked to hundreds of carers, both family and professional, on local and national helplines as well as at meetings, workshops and conferences, since her adult daughter, who is now well, was diagnosed with anorexia nervosa, binge/purge type – discussions she frequently quotes from in her non-fiction books for home carers.

Anna Crane is a general practitioner and has personal experience of living with an eating disorder at medical school. She has written about her experiences in the *Student BMJ*. She is keen to raise the profile of eating disorders in primary care and improve curriculum coverage for GPs in training. She gives sessions on diagnosing and supporting patients with eating disorders in general practice to GPs and junior doctors.

Skills-based Caring for a Loved One with an Eating Disorder

The new Maudsley method
Second edition

Janet Treasure, Gráinne Smith
and Anna Crane

Routledge
Taylor & Francis Group

LONDON AND NEW YORK

Second edition published 2017
by Routledge
2 Park Square, Milton Park, Abingdon, Oxon OX14 4RN

and by Routledge
711 Third Avenue, New York, NY 10017

Routledge is an imprint of the Taylor & Francis Group, an informa business

Typeset in TheSans by Wearset Ltd, Boldon, Tyne and Wear

First edition published by Routledge 2007

British Library Cataloguing in Publication Data
A catalogue record for this book is available from the British Library

Library of Congress Cataloging in Publication Data
Names: Treasure, Janet, editor. | Smith, Gráinne, 1945, editor. |
Crane, Anna, editor.
Title: Skills-based caring for a loved one with an eating disorder: the new
Maudsley method/edited by Janet Treasure, Gráinne Smith and Anna Crane.
Other titles: Skills-based learning for caring for a loved one with an eating
disorder
Description: Second edition. | Abingdon, Oxon; New York, NY: Routledge,
2016. | Preceded by Skills-based learning for caring for a loved one with an
eating disorder: the new Maudsley method/Janet Treasure, Gráinne Smith
and Anna Crane. 2007.
Identifiers: LCCN 2015041195 | ISBN 9781138826649 (hardback) |
ISBN 9781138826632 (pbk.) | ISBN 9781315735610 (e-book)
Subjects: | MESH: Eating Disorders–therapy. | Family Therapy–methods.
Classification: LCC RC552.E18 | NLM WM 175 | DDC 616.85/26–dc23
LC record available at http://lccn.loc.gov/2015041195

ISBN: 978-1-138-82664-9 (hbk)
ISBN: 978-1-138-82663-2 (pbk)
ISBN: 978-1-315-73561-0 (ebk)

Contents

Preface

Why have we written this manual?

Eating disorder symptoms have a profound impact on both people with eating disorders and those who care for them. Often the impacts on carers have been neglected.

Explaining current eating disorder research may help carers understand the basis for altered thinking and behaviours in sufferers.

Automatic reactions to these symptoms, however well intentioned, may not be the most helpful.

Taking a step back to reflect on the most effective way to manage symptoms can lessen the adverse impact on you as a family and the individual.

Practical skills helpful in home management are the same as those used by professionals on specialised eating disorders units, such as the Maudsley.

For example, our work with carers suggests that several 'C' words can be useful cues to keep in mind, to create consistent, coord-inated all-round care: calmness, communication, compassion, cooperation, collaboration to ensure consistency, and coaching.

This book therefore gives you skills and information about working with the current Maudsley method.

Our research suggests that fathers in particular benefit from this approach by helping them to step into a more active role when they put the tips into practice.

Over many years, our ward teams at the Maudsley have developed vast expertise and skills to help eating disorder sufferers. Our aim is to summarise and share some of this information. We hope that you too can become competent in helping someone with an eating disorder to recover.

> **FACT – As a carer you CAN have a role in preventing the illness from retaining its hold over an individual's life. We hope this manual will provide you with the know-how.**

Who are we?

Janet Treasure OBE, PhD, FRCP, FRCPsych is a psychiatrist who has worked professionally with people with eating disorders for over 33 years at the Eating Disorder Unit at the South London and Maudsley Hospital NHS Trust, which is a leading centre in clinical management and academic research of eating disorders. She was chairman of the physical treatment section of the UK NICE guideline committee. She is the Chief Medical Advisor for B-eat (the main UK eating disorder charity). She was awarded with a leadership for research with the Academy of Eating Disorders in 2007 and was also awarded a lifetime achievement award from the Academy of Eating Disorders and from Beat in 2014. She is trustee of the charities Student Minds, Charlotte's Helix, Diabetics with Eating Disorders and the Psychiatry Research Trust and is on the scientific board of the charities Succeed, MAED – Mothers Against Eating Disorders and F.E.A.S.T.

A former head teacher, for many years, **Gráinne Smith** cared for and supported her daughter through anorexia nervosa, binge-purge type – initially with no information or support (unfortunately, a common tale for home carers at the time). Later, for several years she helped start and ran a helpline for carers in Scotland and beyond, then worked on EDA (now Beat UK) telephone helpline. Until recently, Gráinne worked with the Open University in Scotland as part of a Carer and Service User Development Group, helping to build training courses for the Social Work Honours Degree. In all her work for family and home caregivers, she often quotes from the real-life stories of carers she has talked to on helplines, at conferences and workshops, and in her books for home carers – *Anorexia and Bulimia in the Family* (John Wiley and Sons, 2004); a book about how to build good all-round communication, *Families, Carers and Professionals: Building Constructive Conversations* (John Wiley and Sons, 2007); and *Surviving Family Care Giving: Coordinating effective care through collaborative communication* (Routledge, 2015). On her website (www.grainnesmith.co.uk), Gráinne has started making a series of podcasts, again often featuring quotes from real-life stories of carers she has talked to at self-help group meetings, workshops and conferences and on helplines.

Anna Crane is a general practitioner and has personal experience of living with an eating disorder at medical school. She has written about her experiences in the *Student BMJ*. She has developed materials for increasing eating disorder awareness.

Elise Pacquette (illustrator) has contributed illustrations to *Anorexia Nervosa: A Survival Guide* and more recently to the second edition of *Getting Better Bite by Bite*.

Elise has managed to recover and sees part of the reason she developed anorexia stemming from concerns about growing up and becoming independent. With this in mind, Elise has created a unique course supporting parents/carers together with their 11–12 year olds to help them understand what it is like to grow up and become independent in today's culture; the course runs in schools as an after-school club. The six-session course covers subjects such as: making the most of who you are, emotions, building good relationships, internet and mobile phone use and resilience, as well as finance and rights and responsibilities in society, forming a firm foundation for further discussion at home in a fun and informative environment. Elise would also like to add that, despite at the time, through treatment, she might have given some carers, both professional and family, a tough time, Elise would like to say to each and every one of them, it was worth your hard work, thank you, I couldn't have become me without your support.

We have also had help and advice from others with lived experience, in particular Sara Moss.

Who can help? Who is a carer?

The word carer is used throughout this book to mean any family member or close friend who offers support. In the main, parents take on this role in the community; however, partners and siblings may also play an invaluable role. Men, fathers, brothers and partners play a key role. Armed with the knowledge and skills taught in this book their role as a wise mentor is invaluable. The content of this book applies to any individual in a caregiving relationship with someone with an eating disorder, both professional and non-professional.

As the information in this book is used for staff training at the specialised eating disorder unit at the Maudsley Hospital, at times the style of the book may not fit exactly with carers' individual situations. Carers may need to adapt the information through discussion before use. However, the broad concepts for practical care, whether in a ward or home situation, are relevant.

What is in a name?

Some people advocate using specific terms – anorexia nervosa or bulimia nervosa or binge eating disorder – but an individual can move in and out and between these different diagnoses.

Therefore, it may be easier to use the broad term 'eating disorder'. Time plays an important role in the complexity of the illness as the symptoms themselves, such as prolonged starvation or abnormal patterns of eating, can produce changes in the brain that produce new symptoms. It therefore may be more accurate to think of different stages of illness – an early phase when symptoms are more fluid and a later enduring phase when symptoms become more stuck and less easy to change.

In writing of these illnesses, it often feels awkward to repeatedly write 'the individual with the eating disorder' or 'your loved one' or 'your daughter, son or spouse'. Rather than use any of these, 'Edi' is used as a name to represent any eating-disordered individual throughout this manual. 'Edi' may be male or female and of any age but, as a carer, substitute your own loved one's name for Edi.

Eating disorders, by their nature, are characterised by extreme and complex behaviours. Trying to come to terms with such behaviour is a huge challenge for carers. Using 'Edi' as a name, instead of William, Sarah, Emily, Laura, etc., may help separate this unacceptable behaviour (sometimes referred to as the anorexic voice or the 'anorexic minx'!) from the person with an eating disorder.

How can you use this training material?

The manual consists of a series of 15 chapters, each of which addresses a topic pertinent to the care of an eating disorder sufferer. Chapter 1 is useful information for the sufferer themselves. Chapters 2 to 15 contain a mix of:

- background information about eating disorders
- examples of situations you may encounter
- practical skills and tips
- tasks to help you put new skills into practice
- 'skills' sheets which can be worked through or 'dipped' in and out of.

The aim of the manual is to guide the carer through the challenges and issues commonly arising, in our experience, from their role. It is up to each individual how they choose to work through this manual. Some may like to skim read the whole text first, going back to relevant chapters pertinent to their situation at the time. Others may prefer to methodically work through each chapter in succession, absorbing each skill in turn. The choice is yours.

Learning new skills

In order to help manage the complex set of problems that an eating disorder presents, you will probably need some new skills. These are skills to (1) break habits, (2) fight fears and (3) develop good all-round communication. These are core skills used by health professionals and take years of training, practice and supervision to master. We have found that most carers are either willing to try to use the skills themselves or find it helpful to understand the rationale for what the professional services are trying to do and can provide much needed support.

1 Breaking harmful habits

The process of breaking harmful habits involves three components: awareness, precise planning and taking action (remembered with the acronym APT). Look out for the icons throughout the chapters.

A indicates awareness. What can I learn from my observations? Awareness and reflection is essentially gathering information and gaining knowledge.

Awareness. This awareness icon asks you to take a different perspective – maybe to see yourself as others see you. Jot down notes and collect information about aspects of behaviour and triggers in the environment that you might miss and neglect because they run on autopilot. Have a reflective listening conversation with someone you trust (see Chapter 8 Communication). Ask for feedback from family and close others on how you are doing.

P stands for precise planning and preparation. Habits and learned behaviours can kick in automatically and take on a life of their own unless they are interrupted early. Have a well-rehearsed and visualised plan to break unhelpful habits. To build the best care possible for Edi, try to make sure other key players are involved in this stage.

Planning. This precise planning icon is a nudge to spend time practising and planning in detail. Brainstorm solutions to overcome obstacles (for example, using if-then scenarios). It helps if you say it out loud, maybe to your phone memo or to a trusted other.

T for try it or take action. Choose a challenge. What do you expect to learn? We learn by surprising our brain with something new.

Try it (and then, try it again). Take the leap – then put your plans into action again and again (at least seven times) in order for it to be wired in. Not every attempt will be successful, but keep at it! Learning new actions will take time, patience and repetition, but it can be done.

Then back to A to build awareness of about what has happened, what went well and what went wrong, what needs further planning and preparation and action.

APT is a continuous process. Trying something new needs to be followed by taking time to review, take stock and reflect. What did you experience? What help would you need to implement or sustain these changes? Can you ask someone else to add their perspective and make some suggestions?

Not only does change have the potential to weaken eating disorder symptoms but it also demonstrates to Edi that you are ready to make changes and therefore hopefully lead by example. It also teaches you how difficult the process of change is. This process is a 'three for one' (weakening the illness, leading by example and developing personal insight)…

2 Fight fears

Fighting fears involves having the courage to feel the fear, and yet going on to see it through. The secret is to divide the task into mini tasks – a ladder of more challenging steps, big enough to be a challenge and not so overwhelming that you become over aroused. It takes time and repetition to consolidate the new learning.

3 Communication

Accurate listening and positive responding are wonderful gifts for anyone. Again it takes time and practice.

Reflection boxes at the end of each chapter summarise important 'take home' messages to contemplate. However, individuals' reflections will be different. What can *you* learn? Monitoring your behaviours with a diary can be a useful window into self-observation. We all benefit from some form of regular feedback as to how we are doing. Can you keep some sort of tally? Have you the courage to be open and share your reflections with someone else, and get an independent progress monitor?

It is not easy to attain the skills we describe in the manual. However, they are useful life skills that can be applied in many situations. Also you can be more effective at helping to change eating-disordered behaviour if you yourself have gone through the process of making changes in your own behaviour.

Will it work? What evidence is there?

As medicine moves from an art into science, professionals now expect that treatments will be evidence based. You may ask what we mean by this. In essence, the question that researchers and clinicians must ask is whether an intervention has been shown to benefit patients. The most robust evidence comes from randomised trials which are large enough to give convincing results. However, the question of whether a treatment works is more complex than this alone – it is important to think about individual differences of each sufferer. In other words, we must consider individual features of each patient, their experiences, their responses and reactions to their individual eating disorder.

Eating disorders spread over critical developmental periods and persist for over ten years on average. Moreover, the form, impact and response to treatment varies. (Thus family-based therapy works very well in the early phase of the illness but less well as the illness becomes more entrenched.) Also patient preferences vary – if the individual drops out of treatment, the intervention cannot work. Thus treatment for people with an eating disorder is not a one size fits all affair, rather it requires 'bespoke tailoring'. There still needs to be judgement about matching treatment for the individual.

There are many research papers which suggest that giving information and skills to the caregivers of people with eating disorders reduces their own distress and burden. Also, there is a great deal of high-quality information which demonstrates how involving the family early in the course of the illness can prevent progress into a severe and enduring form of illness.

There is much less information about how caregivers can help in the situation where the habits have become more entrenched into a form of adult identity. The skills outlined in this book are designed to help in this more difficult situation. There is some preliminary evidence from two studies that have found that the patients themselves comment positively on the change in the relationship when parents and other home carers follow some of the tips and advice given in this book. Moreover, the strength of the eating disorders also lessened and there was less need to use hospital care.

We continue to modify the materials as we learn more and we have had help from the charity Succeed to produce audiovisual materials to supplement this book (www.succeedfoundation. org). Therefore, we believe there is good evidence to support the use of these materials. In addition to teaching these skills to family caregivers, many centres across the world are now using these materials as training for nurses in specialised units.

Tips to success

1 Building skills

Awareness, Planning and Practice (Try It), facing fears and good communication are fundamental components to successfully using this manual. *It cannot be emphasised enough how important it is to keep learning and practising.*

The training of a professional therapist takes years and involves continued support and feedback sessions in the form of tutorials with other more experienced professionals (known as 'supervision'). Training requires listening to audio or videotapes of performances/presentations and constant reflection, analysis and documentation of progress and errors. Obviously, this is not easy to transfer to the home situation … Try to set aside time to reflect on your progress. If possible, ask for feedback from your partner, from a relative or friend, and from the person with the eating disorder – Edi.

Is it possible to get some support from other carers, perhaps through a self-help group?

2 The process

This training package will help you to appreciate that it is the process – *how* and *what* you do – rather than any single outcome from an interaction that is important. Keep this in mind.

3 'Every mistake is a treasure'

As in other areas of life, mistakes will be made throughout the process, and it is vitally important to remember that they should not be viewed as failures. Do not let high personal standards or perfectionism cramp your new style. In fact, mistakes can be viewed as learning opportunities for you and your loved one by demonstrating that no person or process can be perfect. You have to make mistakes in order to get to the optimal path for you – no mistakes may mean too much avoidance. Throughout the manual, you will be reminded of this.

And finally

It is not possible to give examples of every problem you might encounter, but we hope that you can adapt some of the broad models that we give you.

We have developed this book with the help of many carers who have told us what their needs are and what works and does not work. There may be errors, so please accept our apologies for these. We are always interested to improve on what we have done.

1

Shared perspectives – lived experience of an eating disorder

Why read on?

You may have been handed this book by your family or a friend; page open, on this chapter. Or you may have found this book for yourself or have followed a recommendation. Whatever has brought you here, whatever your present circumstances, and however long or short your journey so far, your feelings are mixed but personal to you – *hoping* that someone will recognise, open their eyes, to your plight; *dismayed* and *angered* that others believe you are ill; *captivated* by your secret, your crutch to life and your 'successful' coping tool; *terrified* of your behaviour and *ashamed* of its consequences and impact on others. Whoever you are, whatever you feel and no matter how strong, ambivalent or indeed irresolute your desire to change is, you must *trust*. Trust that at some point, somewhere and somehow, you will *need* someone to help you. YOU have to want to get through this but, however much of a self-sufficient island and free agent you profess to be, remember that *'you alone can do it, but you can't do it alone'*.

This book aims to enlighten those closest to you, maybe your husband, a friend, a parent or a sibling, as to how to guide and support you through your eating disorder. The techniques and information contained here have been built on over time, from three perspectives – knowledgeable professional, experienced carer and recovering sufferer.

There is nothing stopping you from reading this book and also becoming your own carer. Or you can show the book to your friends or therapist and work with it this way.

We encourage you to explore additional ways this book could be helpful. Perhaps you could share it with your friends or therapist. You could even read portions of it yourself. First, it may be helpful to briefly summarise the topics covered, so you understand the approach your carer may choose to take. Additionally, you may begin to appreciate the ways that having an informed and skilled carer can help you to start or continue on your journey. We find that once carers recognise how hard it is to change their own behaviour, they have more sympathy for your struggles.

A snapshot

1 Animal metaphors

Eating disorder symptoms have a profound impact on those close to you as well as you, the sufferer. Your eating disorder behaviour may prompt a whole host of reactions – anger, frustration, despair, tears, panic, anxiety or even ignorance. In Chapter 5, we ask carers to identify and acknowledge how they respond to eating disorder symptoms. We have created a set of animal metaphors that describe ways carers commonly respond to loved ones with eating disorders. Consider whether any of these patterns are similar to the way your carer(s) responds to your eating disorder.

Do they smother you with protection, safeguarding your every movement? Do they treat you as an invalid or an incapable child, unable to make decisions for yourself? In other words, are they like a *Kangaroo* – with you sheltered and hidden in a pouch?

Do they charge in with anger and irritation? Do they not understand why you behave as you do: 'Just eat more, there – simple!' or

'Stop visiting the bathroom after meals; problem solved'. In other words, are they like a *Rhino*, with rage and control being the only two solutions they have?

Maybe they act like a *Terrier*, constantly going on, criticising and questioning you about food and eating?

You may find that your carer chooses to ignore your deteriorating health, damaging habits and self-destructive nature. Might it be too painful, too frightening or too real for them to watch? Do they bury their head in the sand, like an *Ostrich*, hoping for time to pass, hoping that all the problems will simply disappear?

Or perhaps they are reduced to tears by your behaviour – touchy and emotionally unstable, like a *Jellyfish*, carrying both immense guilt and shame for the conviction that they are to blame for 'all of this'.

These emotional reactions can make carers frightened to help you tackle your eating disorder behaviours. We discuss this pattern of accommodation to the illness in Chapters 5 and 13. Carers need broad shoulders and a wise head to calmly support you to make changes.

We explain in Chapters 9 and 13 that these reactions, although natural and instinctive, are universally unhelpful: both to the rest of your family and to you in coping with your eating disorder. We aim to provide carers with the tools, skills and knowledge to change their response; to work with you rather than against you; to hasten recovery, life and health rather than protract your illness, demise and ruin; and to challenge and weaken your eating disorder rather than strengthen and reinforce it. A carer changing their behaviour may help you to realise that change is possible and not insurmountable.

2 The facts

Chapters 2 and 3 aim to educate carers about eating disorders – dispelling common myths and improving their ability to recognise symptoms (Chapter 2) and acknowledging the potential medical risk and health consequences involved (Chapter 3). It may also be useful for you to read these chapters. You will realise just how unaware and blind the general population is to disordered eating and, importantly, the potential risks and consequences to health, and life, your illness presents for you. Additionally, by sharing common beliefs, you and your carers are working *together* from a joint perspective, the importance of which can never be underestimated.

We also describe the particularly noxious aspects of these illnesses – the scary symptoms which cause loss of the nutrients essential to life and which damage your body and brain. The damage to the brain is particularly problematic because it is the main resource needed to foster recovery. With poor nutrition, thought patterns become distorted, which is one of the main reasons you will probably need help from others to make this journey (and one of the important reasons to write this book).

3 Change

Chapter 7 outlines the different stages of change recognised in sufferers. Perhaps you can identify with the text and the diagram on p. 71? A carer needs to appreciate that *you* have to want to change – only you can make the decision that you want life, health and a future. Remember, '*you alone can do it*'. No amount of bullying, coercion, deception or force can sway you if you are determined to stick with the illness. However, from Chapter 7, carers learn that they have a role in the process of change, giving you time, opportunity and encouragement to express the pros and the cons of changing. You need this. As always remember that 'You can do it – but *you can't do it alone*'. Furthermore, using the 'Readiness Ruler' described in the chapter gives you a useful concrete marker of your progress.

4 Communication

Communication – an essential part in the process to recovery – is the focus of Chapter 8. You might feel that no one listens to you or that other people in the house just don't 'get you'. Perhaps it seems like no one recognises how hard you struggle or comments when you do succeed and achieve. Good communication is hard to perfect, especially when a pattern of strained relationships and resentment has developed in a household. Chapter 8, through sequential Communication Skills topics, gives a carer the resources to steer you towards health in the long term and, in the short term, improve home life, atmosphere and family relationships.

5 Lost emotions

It can be very challenging to understand the emotional underpinnings of your eating disorder – does it seem like it is 'just' about weight, 'just' about calories, exercise and what you see when you look in the mirror? Or are you aware of how your eating disorder dulls, 'takes the edge off' and controls strong emotions and intense feelings? Whatever your present stance, take a moment to read the following. This sufferer writes of her relationship with her anorexia nervosa, aptly named by her as 'Ed', on entering inpatient treatment:

> Nurses put up with my outbursts, my anger, my tears, my frustration and my screams as two years of repressed feelings and emotions poured out uncontrollably. They let me fight, they let me cry and they let me grieve for the loss of my so-called 'friend'. Ed squashes all emotions – good and bad. With Ed, there is no anger, no laughter, no rage, no joy, no sadness, no pleasure, no anxiety, no pain, just numbness. No feelings at all, nothing. Ed is a barrier and a protector. With Ed, you feel untouchable, invisible and immune. Gradually, after weeks of treatment my feelings started to flow – so intense and unmanageable at first. My emotions were extreme, frightening, unknown and so quick to change. Calmness could evolve into terror, laughter into shame within moments. Tears rolled down my face at every

opportunity. The more I engage with life, the more I learn about how to manage these alien feelings. The numbness that Ed creates blocks out everything. With an eating disorder, a sufferer misses out on all the amazing emotions that life brings, just so that they can escape the painful emotions. Treatment teaches a sufferer the tools they need to tackle life along with its resulting emotions.

Other eating behaviours such as bingeing, over-exercising and vomiting may also be a way of trying to soothe or distract from intense feelings. Or maybe you feel constantly physically 'full'; enormous, like a balloon, taut and stretched, and unable to fill yourself up anymore? Try and reconsider this. Perhaps you are full of suppressed and unvented feelings and emotions? Maybe you relieve this 'fullness' by restricting what you eat or perhaps you purge or vomit?

Identifying and discussing emotions is difficult for many people and families (even those without eating disorders). In fact, sometimes it seems taboo to talk about feelings at all. This may mean that no one has ever asked how you feel before or that you have trouble recognising or identifying your emotions. The best way to learn is often by example; Chapter 11 coaches a carer on how to be 'emotionally intelligent', an important skill to grasp.

6 Lost connections

The eating disorder may have led to you becoming disconnected from those you love. Chapter 10 focuses on social communication, including how the eating disorder can affect your relationships with partners, friends and siblings. Isolation and loneliness are highly toxic for the human social animal – and this stress can further damage your mind and body. The understanding and skills in this book can repair these ruptures in relationships. This is the first step to becoming more connected with the world.

7 Eating and behaviour

Chapters 12 and 13 deal with aspects of eating (undereating and overeating) and Chapter 14 addresses other additional problem behaviours. Do you have strict rules regarding food? For example, 'to be eaten, food has to be earned, deserved and worked hard for' or 'food must be kept separate; no mixing of proteins, carbohydrates or vegetables'. You might be able to identify with some of the rules on pp. 167? These rules might be used to keep you 'safe' after eating, such as exercising, vomiting or using laxatives? To break free from your eating disorder, you also need to break free from such behaviours and rules, which can sometimes seem like one of the scariest or most difficult aspects of recovery. Chapter 12 explains how a carer can help you obtain distance and separation from these rules; through conversation and weighing up the pros and cons (p. 179); through 'naming and shaming' your personal rules (p. 195); and by using an ABC approach (p. 185). Furthermore, however resistant you may be to change or to help, practical suggestions of how a carer is to assist you best at mealtimes and with food are described. *'You can't do it alone'* is particularly apt in terms of eating. Chapter 13 explains how dangerous patterns with food can build up in your brain so that you are beset by intense cravings, and also describes how changes in the environment can help a dysregulated appetite system.

There may be aspects of your behaviour which other people in the house find very difficult to cope with – e.g. vomiting, isolating and bingeing. There may also be aspects of behaviour which you, yourself, find tough or tiring to cope with – e.g. cleaning rituals, cooking rituals and constant negative self-ruminations. Perhaps you are ready or willing to change certain behaviours but more reluctant to alter those which provide you with the greatest degree of 'safety'? In Chapter 14, carers can learn techniques for guiding and supporting you through the process of relinquishing problem behaviours.

We teach carers the APT cornerstones of working to change habits (see Preface).

These include first AWARENESS, bringing the behaviours to conscious attention and reflection by recording the when, how and what about them in a journal and using this process to keep track of progress.

Second, PLANNING. You need to prepare 'if ... then ... Scenarios' to help you in deciding what to change, how to do it, who will support you, etc. Using visualisation (having a story board like in a film) and vocalisation (talking it through) to foresee all the potential problems is helpful. You need to prepare for the time when you will automatically wire in healthy habits.

Finally, TRYING the new behaviour and going through the loop again and again. What have you learned? Can you reflect on the process of trying the new behaviour? You need to give it a go for a minimum of seven times. Remember, mistakes will be made – *everyone* sometimes makes mistakes! – and that every mistake is a treasure. If you had a goal that was too difficult (or even too easy), you can try again.

Collected thoughts

What has been the response from sufferers whose carers have undertaken this approach?

- **Reassurance:** 'I felt they (my parents) became "lighter" and "freer" somehow. It gave them comfort that other people face the same issues, the same problems and same challenges. They were then less stressed around me.'

- **Solving isolation:** 'It was like, for years, they (my parents) were just trapped with me in my illness. They wouldn't leave me on my own, wouldn't go on holiday, out to the cinema or anywhere. The whole family just lived through and focused on my eating disorder. It was like we were all trapped in a bubble. The book, I think, gave them scope to look outside the illness in addition to caring; to take time just for them, to do things they enjoyed and to live their lives, instead of living everything through me and my illness.'

- **Revealed secrets:** 'Up until my Mum began to learn more about eating disorders, mine was a secret. It was private and just for me. I was devious and, wow, I was good at it! Somehow, her knowledge "exposed" my illness. She'd read the tricks and she knew my deceptive ways. The illness became not so individual and not so personal. Somehow a barrier was broken down. I was furious to begin with but, in retrospect, it was the only way for me to start the recovery process.'

- **Understanding:** 'What's in your head is really complex for others to understand. They just don't get the fear, the guilt and the self-repulsion. It's all so inconceivable. They (my parents) weren't aware of the feelings behind my illness. For them, initially it was about the food – about getting me to eat more or keeping as much down me as possible. They started to realise, after reading, that it was so much more than this – sensitivity, repressed feelings, personality types, self-esteem, interpreting social interactions, etc. Their response to me changed totally.'

- **Whose decision is it anyway?:** 'I think my Mum realised that if my life was going to change, I had to want it to. She left more decisions up to me and gave me extra responsibilities. It was hard not to abuse her trust at times but the guilt and sense of shame I had if I did, was unbearable. I think if she hadn't have "taken a back seat" then I would just have stayed stuck for years.'

- **Reality check:** 'By this stage I'd decided that I wanted to change. I'd discussed the pros and the cons of my illness with my parents so many times. I knew them all so well! The frustrating thing was that whenever food was involved, my world narrowed. I just couldn't see that I had future plans, hopes and aspirations. All I could see was what was on the plate in front of me. They reminded me of the "real world" and the "bigger picture" at mealtimes. It got me through.'

ACTION POINTS ➤

- If you can find the courage to read this book, you will have taken the first step to being able to see beyond your eating disorder to the bigger life that will be in store for you without it.

- You will be able to gain a new perspective – what it might be like for others looking on.

- Being able to take an overview about your own and others' thinking, emotions, sensations, memories and perceptions is a large leap to mature wisdom.

 # REFLECTION POINTS

1. *'You alone can do it, but you can't do it alone'* – in this book we try to share with carers some of the understanding that can help them feel less perplexed by this illness and more able to cope.

2. Secrets are not helpful. Openness and respect are key components for recovery. This book lays bare some of the confusion about eating disorders.

3. *'Every mistake is a treasure'* – mistakes can teach us a lot, and make us think about what went wrong and how to change things and do better next time.

2

Working with a joint understanding of the illness – basic facts about eating disorders

The five most common questions about *any* illness are:

1. What are the symptoms?

2. What are the causes?

3. What is the expected time course?

4. What are the consequences (a) for the sufferer, (b) for close others?

5. How controllable/treatable is the illness?

Is this an eating disorder?

With so many people on a diet, how do you know it is not just a passing phase? The first signs of an eating disorder are subtle and are often meticulously concealed by a sufferer. Behaviours may begin over many years and are often misconstrued as just 'normal' growing up or perceived as a change in hobbies, interests or concerns. The 'classic' emaciated appearance of a sufferer triggers immediate alarm bells and a spot diagnosis but, when body weight is 'normal', to detect an eating disorder requires looking deeper, beyond physicalities.

In Table 2.1, there are some pointers that can alert you to the fact that something more serious than dieting is involved. Someone developing an eating disorder may have several of the signs shown in Table 2.1.

TABLE 2.1   Distinguishing Normal Dieting from Eating Disorder Symptoms

- Denial of diet – dieters talk about it all the time
- Change in food rules, e.g. becoming vegetarian
- Denial of hunger and craving
- Covering up the weight loss, possibly by wearing baggy clothes
- Increased interest in food – cooking for others, scouring recipe books, supermarket shelf gazing and calorie counting
- Claims of needing to eat less than others or only very small portions
- Eating slowly, with small mouthfuls
- Avoiding eating with others, e.g. the excuse of having eaten already or eaten elsewhere
- Behaviour becoming more compulsive and ritualised – cleaning, tidying, organising, washing, etc.
- Forming rigid rules about eating: only certain foods, brands, times of day
- Becoming socially isolated and low in mood
- Frequently disappearing to the bathroom – during meals and after; the smell of vomit or excessive use of air fresheners about the house
- Self-criticism – dissatisfaction with physical appearance and general achievements, personality and social capabilities; self-deprecating comments such as 'I'm rubbish', 'I'm such a bitch', 'I'm stupid', 'I'm lazy', 'I'm such a freak' and 'I'm so useless at that'
- A new or increased exercise routine – strict, rigid and gruelling
- Irritability/anger if confronted about eating behaviour or exercise

Common myths about eating disorders

Although general 'eating disorder information' is applicable to most sufferers, there are also unique aspects to every case. Mistaken assumptions about the illness can lead to unhelpful intervention strategies. This in turn will cause distress, not just to the sufferer, but also to family and friends.

In the following section, we give just a few examples of some common mistaken assumptions. You probably have your own beliefs – which may, or may not, be helpful in coping with the illness.

- *'Families (in particular mothers) are responsible for their daughter/son developing an eating disorder.'*
- *'People with eating disorders choose to have their illness. They want to be ill/to die/to not grow up.'*
- *'People with eating disorders are trying to punish their parents, or whoever they live with.'*
- *'Families with an eating disorder in their midst need therapy.'*
- *'Eating disorders are all to do with vanity and aspirations to be a model.'*
- *'It's just another form of teenage attention-seeking behaviour and rebellion.'*
- *'It's something that people grow out of, a passing phase.'*
- *'The person is cured, completely, after a period of inpatient treatment.'*
- *'You must do all you can to please and humour the person who is ill.'*
- *'The hospital and treatment team can always cure them.'*
- *'It is just a question of eating.'*
- *'People with eating disorders know what to eat; they just choose not to.'*
- *'Eating disorders are just extreme diets.'*
- *'Once you have an eating disorder, you can never recover.'*
- *'Once the individual reaches a healthy weight, they are cured.'*

When family members or anyone else hold beliefs like these, negative emotions such as guilt, remorse, anger, frustration and recrimination flourish, leading to increased stress and tension. To date, evidence for the causes of eating disorders is patchy, with much scientific research still focused on the area. Many written sources contain myths about the illness which can be hurtful and unhelpful.

What is known is that an eating disorder is not just a problem with eating and food. There are deeper issues relating to identity, emotions, beliefs and values. Treatment can take time, and some aspects of recovery take place within the context of normal development. A journey towards recovery is often long and challenging, but beating an eating disorder can be achieved.

Facts so far...

In an ideal situation, everyone – sufferer, family members and health professionals – would be working from the same understanding of eating disorders, with information based on research evidence. Important knowledge, beliefs and attitudes are best shared to enable collaboration and teamwork. This is not always easy to achieve in practice because there is a great deal of conflicting information about eating disorders. These differing perspectives and evidence do support an important principle: *there does not seem to be any one clear cause*. We hope that the following information provides a solid, foundational understanding based on high-quality, widely accepted research findings.

What factors contribute to the development of eating disorders?

Biological factors

Recent research suggests that many of the mechanisms that underlie eating disorders are not under conscious or wilful control. Rather, a network of biological systems – including the way that the brain processes information, emotions and behaviours – contributes to the illness. Some of these factors are fixed and are related to genes, whereas others emerge from environment and upbringing. However, the way that genes and behaviour are connected is unknown at the present time.

Key research findings[1]

- Genetic factors account for over 50 per cent of the risk in eating disorders.

- Often, though not always, an eating disorder develops at or around puberty, which is a phase of complex brain maturation/development. This timing can create a self-perpetuating trap as starvation and learned behaviours interrupt this developmental process, making recovery more difficult.

- People with eating disorders have been found to have a chemical imbalance in their brain. Receptors for serotonin and dopamine – both key signalling chemicals which play a role in mood and appetite – are reduced both in the acute state of illness and after recovery.

- Brain scans have revealed that when people with eating disorders are shown food-related cues, their brains respond in unusual ways. More specifically, the front of the brain (which is involved in decision making and emotional regulation) also becomes activated. This suggests that the *meaning* and *reaction* to food becomes entangled with regulation of motivation and planning.

Emotional and cognitive factors

Emotional and thinking dispositions appear to be of relevance in eating disorders. These characteristics may be innate, or may develop as part of the illness process.

Key research findings

- People with eating disorders tend to be more sensitive than others to perceived threat. For example, they are more likely to find starting a new school year, or staying over with friends, more frightening than other people.

- Often people with eating disorders are more conscientious, try harder to please others and do things to a very high standard.

- They may also run into social difficulties, including suddenly getting excluded from a friendship group.

- A thinking style that increases illness risk is one that favours attention to detail with a superior ability to focus. Being able to concentrate and focus on detail can be a great asset – but this thinking style becomes a problem when individuals have trouble being flexible and when the focus becomes so intense that the bigger picture is lost.

  o For example, Edi focuses on food and eating to the exclusion of everything else (e.g. school/work/friends/social activities, etc.), including health.

- Also Edi may have a predisposition to develop automatic habits – which can be great for learning, but if those automatic habits are not healthy this can be very physically destructive.

These figures illustrate how eating disorder symptoms get stuck as a result of the secondary effects of starvation and abnormal eating habits on the brain. This results in fixed and focused habits which are difficult to change.

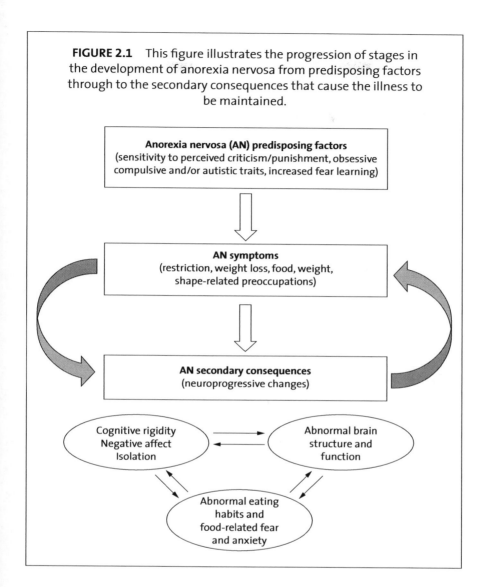

FIGURE 2.1 This figure illustrates the progression of stages in the development of anorexia nervosa from predisposing factors through to the secondary consequences that cause the illness to be maintained.

How are eating disorders treated?

As yet there is little evidence to support any one form of treatment in eating disorders, but forms of psychotherapy – talking treatments – have been found to be the most successful and acceptable. These need to be combined with careful physical monitoring. In some cases, these treatments and monitoring

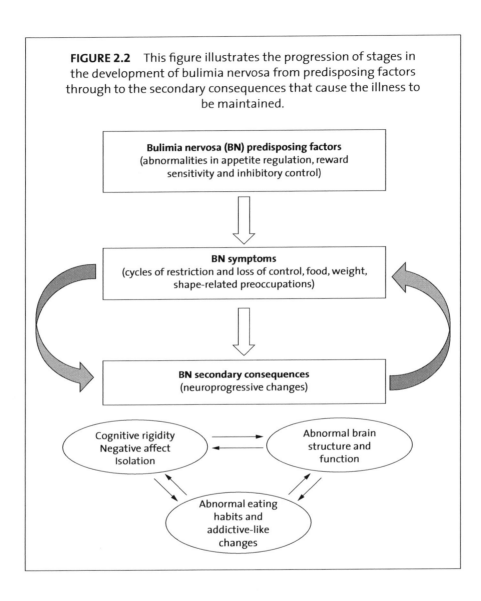

FIGURE 2.2 This figure illustrates the progression of stages in the development of bulimia nervosa from predisposing factors through to the secondary consequences that cause the illness to be maintained.

Bulimia nervosa (BN) predisposing factors
(abnormalities in appetite regulation, reward sensitivity and inhibitory control)

BN symptoms
(cycles of restriction and loss of control, food, weight, shape-related preoccupations)

BN secondary consequences
(neuroprogressive changes)

Cognitive rigidity
Negative affect
Isolation

Abnormal brain structure and function

Abnormal eating habits and addictive-like changes

may be effective through outpatient departments. In other cases, nutritional support is necessary in a specialised hospital unit. Inpatient treatment is usually successful in terms of weight gain in the short term; however, if the individual groundwork in addressing the underlying emotional problems is not done, there is a high chance of relapse.

working with a joint understanding

TABLE 2.2 What can we learn from this?

- These findings argue against the myth that eating disorders are caused by wilful stubbornness on the part of the sufferer.

- Individuals with eating disorders are not on a hunger strike. They are not trying to do something to anyone else. Rather, the symptoms are a marker of deeper levels of stress and distress which leave their imprint on brain function.

- The brain is an adaptive 'plastic' organ, i.e. it can grow and respond to environmental events. Stress and starvation can inhibit this process.

- The longer abnormal amounts of food and nourishment are taken, or patterns of disordered eating (eating too little, eating too much or perhaps getting rid of all nourishment after eating) persist, the more the brain adapts to a high stress and/or addictive state.

- The longer starvation or behaviours continue, the more difficult it is to recover as the brain remains immature.

- In order to promote recovery, individuals with an eating disorder need to learn to practise behaving differently or even to oppose their natural instincts. This process will help form and 'tone up' new brain pathways.

- For many people with eating disorders, e.g. anorexia nervosa, early stages of treatment involve restoration of nutritional health. This is particularly important because starvation interrupts brain development, and so people can be stuck if they remain undernourished for long periods.

- Some medical consequences of starvation, such as the failure of bone development and reproductive function, are reversed by weight gain. Likewise, salt imbalances from laxative overuse and/or vomiting, are reversed during a period of remission. The brain control of appetite is the primary problem and should be the focus of treatment (see Chapter 12 for more details).

- Once weight gain has been achieved, a secondary target is weight maintenance. Can the individual sustain their weight without a high level of external control (e.g. what happens between outpatient treatment appointments, or on weekend leave from hospital care)?

It is also important for people with eating disorders to put in time and effort to get to know themselves, their strengths and weaknesses so that they can create and find an environment in which they will flourish. For example, if you are someone who likes order and planning and likes to solve problems in sequence, you are less likely to flourish in an accident and emergency department or in work with a high level of interaction with the public. However, encourage people to whom order and planning are very important to work in a lab or a library – and works of genius may arise.

People who have recovered from an eating disorder often feel that they are 'behind in life'. They have lost out on years of emotional maturation and life experience as their illness has squashed and restricted their world and thinking. 'Catch up' is possible and often treatment programmes include everyday experiences that peers would take for granted, e.g. going to the cinema, a beach day trip, a pampering session.

Why are eating disorders so difficult to treat?

One of the reasons that people become stuck within an eating disorder is that brain damage resulting from starvation makes it more difficult to change. The brain actively uses calories to think and learn along with all the more unconscious aspects of living – on average 500 calories per day are needed to support brain activity. Without those calories, essential for thinking and working things out, it is much harder to lay down new learning. The brain reaction to starvation is to produce an extreme stress state with little life force.

- Not only is brain function disturbed in many ways by an eating disorder, but the brain size itself is reduced. The most sophisticated aspects of brain function which use larger networks suffer most. These include the areas of the brain involved in social functioning and emotional regulation. (More discussion on this in Chapter 10.) Thus *social emotional*

working with a joint understanding

functioning is reduced, and *flexibility* and *the ability to see the bigger picture* are impaired.

- It is not just the absolute amount of starvation that counts in terms of brain damage, but also how and what is eaten. Neuro-adaptive changes occur if there is a pattern of fasting and feasting, particularly if the feasting consists of highly palatable high sugar and high fat foods (which are common in bingeing).

- Preventing the formation of new negative habits and patterns is very important – once they form they are very difficult to break. Ensuring that there is a regular pattern of eating with a broad range of nutrients can help prevent this cycle developing. Bingeing and overeating is discussed further in Chapter 13.

- In addition, binges produce addictive-like changes in the brain – cravings for this type of food increase, and the impulsive, automatic signals that drive the need to act on these processes also increase.

  o These secondary neuro-adaptive changes become hard-wired, stamp in the changed patterns of eating and isolate the individual.

These factors together cause an illness spiral: starvation produces brain problems, these in turn cause anxiety and stress, problem eating then seems to reduce anxiety in the short term – but in the longer term it produces brain problems. And so the spiral continues. Thus once the starvation has persisted for several years there are many more problems to be overcome.

Correcting malnutrition (whether undereating, or bingeing and purging, or a mix of both) as early as possible in the course of an eating disorder can interrupt this illness spiral.

How long will it last?

The course of an eating disorder is variable. Results from specialist centres suggest that on average the duration is 6–12 years. Thus, if an eating disorder starts in adolescence most people continue to have problems when they are young adults. However, within this range, there are people who recover within a year and others who have an enduring severe course of illness. Although the course of the illness often becomes more complicated over time, no matter how long someone has been ill, recovery is possible.

What is the prognosis?

Because the course of an eating disorder is variable between individuals, so is its prognosis. Some useful points to remember are as follows:

- The outcome of younger cases, or those with a short duration of illness, is good.

- Effective treatment *early* in the course of the illness, which is less than three years, leads to a good outcome in 90 per cent of cases.

  o When the illness fails to respond to several attempts at treatment, very rigid thinking and behaviours are harder to break down and overcome. Nevertheless it is always possible to break away from the illness and attain not only recovery but a state that has been termed 'post traumatic growth' – whereby the deepened self-understanding and skills that are needed to recover from the illness can allow an individual to live a highly meaningful life.

- Restoring weight to a normal level in hospital, by itself, does not ensure that the outcome is good. Understanding and unpicking the association of food and weight issues with emotions, styles of thinking and supportive relationships are essential for effective treatment.

working with a joint understanding

REFLECTION POINTS

1. Myths are unhelpful and hurtful. They reflect attitudes and behaviours towards you, other family members and Edi, as well as increasing stress levels.

2. The development of an eating disorder is *not* under conscious or wilful control.

3. Whilst there is uncertainty about the causes of eating disorders, the consequences are clear. Professionals and family members can modify the consequences by working to decrease the time spent in a severely emaciated or dysregulated state and by coaching the individual to attain mature emotional, cognitive and social development.

 ## ACTION POINT

Dispel your own myths and beliefs about eating disorders by getting information from reliable sources such as the NICE guidelines, Beat or the Academy of Eating Disorders. Share the information with family and friends involved in Edi's care. Try to ensure that everyone is working from the same understanding.

Note

1. We have not included references to the research as the field is changing so quickly they become out of date. There is a move to make the key literature 'open access', which means that you can search perhaps on Google Scholar for what interests you.

Further reading

Schmidt, U, Alexander, J. and Treasure, J. *Getting Better Bite by Bite*. Second Edition. London: Routledge, 2015.

Treasure, J. and Alexander, J. *Anorexia Nervosa: A recovery guide for sufferers, families and friends*. Second Edition. London: Routledge, 2013.

3

Consequences – and awareness of medical risk

Important observations

Most people living with someone with an eating disorder are terrified about the medical dangers, and the long-term and short-term consequences of poor nutrition. As we have already stressed, it is helpful in discussion with medical professionals if you can be specific about what observations worry you. It can also be useful to jot any examples down, with any relevant details, such as how often you have observed this, when it happened, etc. (Hopefully at a later stage you will also be able to look back and appreciate progress.)

Finding a balance between being mindful of the medical risk that your loved one faces, and not panicking over what may or may not be important from a medical point of view, is often very difficult. This chapter offers basic guidance which may be discussed with an experienced professional on what to look out for, what it means and when to call for help.

Body mass index

A term used by health professionals as a measure of weight in all patients, not just those with eating disorders, is Body Mass Index (BMI).

Question: How is BMI calculated?
BMI is a form of volume measurement, so it is calculated by dividing weight in kilograms by the square of height in metres. There are online BMI calculators available.

BMI is one way that healthcare professionals calculate a rough estimate of medical risk.

The World Health Organisation suggests that the underweight criteria for adults with anorexia nervosa is a BMI of less than 18.5 and 'dangerously low body weight' or 'severe thinness' is a BMI less than 16.0. For school-aged children and older adolescents, things are a little more complicated because of growth.

In addition to the absolute measure of BMI, other factors that can contribute to risk include:

- the rate at which weight is falling

- whether behaviours such as the use of laxatives and vomiting are present

- if there are pre-existing medical conditions, e.g. diabetes.

Regular weight monitoring

An important part of the treatment of anorexia nervosa is to monitor medical risk regularly, by measuring weight as a minimal proxy measure of risk. Both professionals and family members should be aware that, during the illness, some sufferers may try to persuade other people that their weight is greater than it actually is by using devious ploys, such as secreting weights/batteries

consequences – and awareness of medical risk

on their person (e.g. in their pockets) or drinking large amounts of liquid before being weighed. Pro-anorexia websites give details of most of these tricks, and sometimes eating-disordered individuals will exchange information on these. Therefore, weight or BMI alone is not a satisfactory measure of risk and a more complex analysis of how the body is functioning is needed. Other important ways to assess risk and monitor health include:

- pulse rate

- blood pressure

- temperature

- muscle strength

- rate of weight loss

- blood tests to check any deficiency in essential nutrients.

This assessment needs to be made by a medical professional who can also carry out regular weight checks. Weight monitoring can be undertaken in a GP surgery by either a GP or by a practice nurse.

All the checks mentioned should be discussed with a sufferer, along with what they mean in relation to their physical health. If the results of these checks place an individual at high risk, then there is a need to reflect about what steps are required to improve their health. A sufferer is the only person who can really take those steps.

Your GP/practice nurse will keep a regular record of Edi's weight fluctuations. You may, for your own security and peace of mind, need to keep your own chart/diary of Edi's weight. This may have a positive or a negative response from Edi depending on the individual and their attitude towards and beliefs about their illness at that point in time. Some sufferers will keep their weekly weights a secret – angry and unwilling to let on whether their illness has won, or not, in terms of the scale's reading.

Others may adopt an open attitude, appreciating their progress by charting and displaying results. Some families and sufferers find home scales beneficial for weight monitoring. For others, Edi's obsession with weight means that scales around the house are unhelpful, distressing and a hindrance to progress. You must work out a weight monitoring system that suits you *and* Edi.

 ACTION

Contact your GP (a note/letter might be easier than the phone, and can be kept for reference with other patient notes) to report any of the following. The sufferer should be medically examined if you notice these symptoms:

- Edi is always so cold that she or he needs the heating on constantly, and/or wears several layers of clothes even when others find it too hot.

- You notice that hands and feet look blue and cold – this is a sign of circulation problems.

- Edi is dizzy and faint after standing up quickly or you notice puffiness around the eyes in the morning, and/or swollen ankles in the afternoon. All of the above can signify salt and water imbalance.

- Edi has difficulty climbing stairs, or brushing their hair, or raising their arms for any length of time. This is due to muscle strength being affected by the illness.

Phone your GP or get emergency help if Edi:

- becomes breathless on lying flat

- develops a very fast heart rate

- has a seizure

- becomes sleepy or twitchy*
- complains of pins and needles in their toes*
- his/her hands twist into a spasm.*

Note: * These indicate serious salt imbalance.

Be cautious at times of particular danger:

- if the routine changes and meals are delayed or missed (e.g. long journeys)
- after excessive exercising
- when starting to feed again – this needs to be taken slowly with small portions of normal food taken at regular intervals throughout the day with vitamin and mineral supplements. At very low weight, a refeeding plan should be discussed with a medical provider.

These are general guidelines. *Your gut feelings are also important* – note anything which concerns you for later discussion.

Important changes – Talking it over with Edi

Skills of positive communication and assertiveness (Chapter 8) are needed when discussing risk with your loved one. This involves:

- voicing your concerns
- stating clearly what action you have taken
- offering to help.

The conversation may go something like this:

> '*I love you/care about you so much … and I've noticed several things which have made me worry about your health. First, you are very sensitive to cold – you have the heater turned on in your room so that it feels like a furnace. Also, I've noticed that you find opening heavy doors difficult. I'd like you to go and have a medical check-up to put my mind at rest. Could I help by making you an appointment with our GP? If you want me to, I'd be happy to come with you.*'

Edi may or may not respond positively to your request for a medical appointment and may try to persuade you to delay an appointment or to minimise your concerns. If there are signs of significant risk, follow through with your instincts. Edi's physical health needs to be a top priority!

The essence is to stay calm but to list your concerns with compassion.

Mental Health Act

The Mental Health Act (MHA) exists to protect people who cannot understand the danger to their health; when this happens a person may be admitted to hospital against their will. Gentle persuasion of the need for specialist hospital care, perhaps trying some of the suggestions in this book such as the 'Readiness Ruler' (see Chapter 7, 'Understanding change'), may work – whereas confrontation may drive Edi further into entrenched resistance.

In very extreme circumstances, after attempts at gentle persuasion, if there is evidence of high medical risk to Edi and their condition has become life-threatening, it may be necessary to use this Act and admit the person to hospital against their will.

Starvation as a maintaining factor

We have outlined how anorexia nervosa can put life acutely in jeopardy because of inadequate nutrition, and in Chapter 2 we describe how starvation can interfere with brain function, making it more difficult to recover from the illness.

Adolescence in particular is a time of important changes in brain function. Developmental changes that occur in a healthy brain include the ability to:

- think abstractly and reflectively

- monitor and put the brakes on automatic aspects of brain function like responding impulsively to novelty, and perceived rewards (e.g. with sex, drugs and rock and roll)

- develop skills in emotional intelligence, including understanding and regulating emotions (both positive and negative).

Poor nutrition during this phase can inhibit these processes, causing the brain to remain in the immature state. Prolonged poor nutrition can freeze brain development, which makes recovery difficult. Similar problems may develop in individuals who develop eating disorders after adolescence; even in these cases you may notice regression in ability to monitor and regulate thoughts and emotions, which highlights the importance of restoring adequate nutrition in a sustained manner as early as is possible in the course of the illness.

Raise awareness

- If you are concerned about Edi's symptoms, jot down examples. When did it happen? For how long? How often? etc.

- Report to your GP, by letter, or phone if urgent, giving relevant details.

- Establish a routine for regular weight monitoring.

- Talk with Edi:

  - Assure of your love and your wish to help if possible.

  - Voice your concerns.

  - Explain your actions.

  - Offer help.

 REFLECTION POINTS

1. Be mindful of risk, and recruit help to manage this if necessary.

2. Prolonged poor nutrition interferes with brain function, impeding recovery.

3. The regulation of emotion, abstract and social intelligence is affected by prolonged poor nutrition, again creating barriers to recovery.

consequences – and awareness of medical risk

4

Caring for a loved one with an eating disorder – first steps

The persistent extreme behaviours associated with eating disorders are frightening and confusing when you first encounter them. You may fear that your loved one has cancer when you see the extreme weight loss. Similarly, persistent vomiting and the distress caused by bingeing is upsetting. Many facets of the symptoms are held in secret. You may have no real idea what is going on – Edi can be very good at concealing disordered eating habits – but your instincts tell you that it is something terrible, with potentially long-term consequences. Recognising that the problem is an eating disorder may be hard for you and even for your general practitioner. Where can you start? The following section may help.

1 Broaching the subject – first thoughts

Chapter 2 explained just how difficult it can be to recognise an eating disorder. Once suspicious, the next step is to encourage Edi to accept that there may be a problem. Remember the APT steps in the Preface (Awareness, Planning, Try It). Use Table 2.1 in Chapter 2 to help with building up your knowledge and awareness of some signs.

People with eating disorders are not easy to help. Some individuals persist with meagre dietary rations, while for others the compulsion to eat breaks down their resolve. They then feel driven to use extreme measures to compensate for their 'indulgence' with over-exercise, vomiting or laxatives. A pattern rather like an addiction can slowly develop, with the individual fasting or subsisting on a monotonous low-calorie diet for long periods; then, suddenly, if a small portion of palatable food passes their lips, being unable to stop eating. Other compulsive, driven behaviours such as over-exercise or quirky rituals can occur. As an observer you may notice that eating behaviours (either too much or too little) are impacting on not only Edi's quality of life, but your life too.

Even though your observations are distressing, you may find it impossible to raise your concerns effectively with Edi as they get brushed aside. One of the core clinical signs of an eating disorder

FIGURE 4.1   Try talking to the real Edi rather than to the illness and squash down the eating disorder bully.

is that the individual perceives some positive benefit to their condition – a sense of well-being, power, control, uniqueness, etc. You may feel frozen and powerless as your loved one becomes angry and/or humiliated when you try to broach the subject. The following sections aim to help you prepare for a conversation with Edi.

A look ahead:

- Chapter 7: Understanding change, and how carers can encourage Edi to move away from behaviour with negative consequences.

- Chapter 9: With eating a core aspect of life, relationships can become fraught both in families and in professional settings. This chapter describes the common reactions to Edi and the strains in the relationship.

- Chapter 10: How social connections and relationships can be damaged by the illness.

---

2 Broaching the subject – preparation and trouble shooting

It can help to prepare yourself and practise for the possible scenarios that might arise when you broach the subject with Edi. Decide *where* and *when* you will introduce the conversation – find a good opportunity when you and Edi are alone together; perhaps a quiet room with no danger of interruption or distraction is best, or perhaps when out for a walk.

In this preparatory phase, it can help to make notes of the possible symptoms and behaviours that have made you feel uneasy. Have these observations to hand when you talk to Edi.

Find as much information about eating disorders as you can and compare your observations with case descriptions. If possible, talk about your concerns with a wise friend.

It takes time for Edi to be able to step aside from the compulsive spirals of thought and action and to be willing or able to listen to your point of view. You need to try to help Edi shift focus from their increasingly narrowed eating/food-driven perspective onto deeper values, such as their health and lifetime ambitions for the future – for example, work, travel, family or friends.

Trouble shooting obstacles – be aware of and try to avoid joining in, and hence encouraging, 'eating disorder talk', such as discussion about food, calories, body shape or weight. These are major preoccupations for the individual – Edi has probably developed detailed knowledge of these topics and is well practised in raising them in conversation. Stepping away from this 'dance' will require you to be reflective and self-disciplined. Getting into an argument will make things worse, so if necessary you can agree to disagree, which hopefully keeps the bridges of communication open for later work. For the interim, bide your time, but remain aware and start to make plans – for instance, think of what you'll say if Edi strongly disagrees with everything you say about disordered eating. For instance, *'I love you so much and my main concern is to see you well. But we don't agree on this. You say ... but I think ..., so let's leave it just now and maybe we can talk about it later. Now I'm going to have a shower/take the dog for a walk/visit a neighbour.'*

Some general preparatory advice is given in Table 4.1.

TABLE 4.1   Planning: A script to broach the subject

- If you are suspicious, **ACT** – **a**sk *gentle* questions, *calmly* express your concern, **t**alk of your observations, reassure of your continuing love and caring.
- Remember – people with eating disorders often reject the idea that they have a problem.
- Don't be shy, don't dismiss or ignore symptoms or give up on the person.
- Let them know that you believe they have a problem. It may be a long while before they themselves can confront and admit that they have a problem.
- Choose your special moments carefully – a relaxed atmosphere is best, away from mealtimes.
- Don't go for browbeating – you don't need to win each battle.
- Be prepared for setbacks, especially initially.

3 Broaching the subject – precise planning

Plan ahead and 'script' a possible interaction. Visualise where, when and with whom. Think carefully of what you want to say about your concerns and imagine Edi's response. As in all things, practice is invaluable, perhaps with another family member or a friend – or even with a mirror.

Try to position yourself as a slightly detached observer, a 'fly on the wall':

> *'I have noticed ... I am concerned about ... Please can you talk to me about it, tell me how you feel...'*

Sometimes thinking of the eating disorder as an anorexic minx or anorexic bully can help you to separate the eating disorder and its behaviour from your loved one. Talk and act as if Edi has mixed feelings about change, as if there are two parts to them: the 'well side' and the 'ill side'. Be calm and compassionate.

Table 4.2 gives some starters to help carers develop their own useful phrases. More are offered throughout the book.

TABLE 4.2 Developing useful phrases

- Normalise mixed feelings:
  'It sounds as if part of you feels…, yet part of you wants to…'
  See Chapter 7 about ambivalence regarding change.

- Describe the facts as you see them calmly and with warmth and offer to help:
  'I see you think … I think you feel … I noticed that … How can I help?'

- Listen carefully to the answers:
  'Sounds like this might be the way you see things…? Have I got that right?'
  Use reflective listening and affirmation to build trust (Chapter 8).

- Find out what, if anything, concerns the person with an eating disorder:
  'The doctor says it would be better to reduce exercising because your BMI is very low. What do you think would have to happen for you to do this?'
  The motivational 'Readiness Ruler' (Chapter 7) is a useful tool.

- Listen without judgement:
  'Everyone has different views. This is not the way I see things; I accept you feel differently.'

- Modulate your emotional reaction, remain *calm and compassionate* (Chapter 11).

- Ask what you and others might be able to do to help:
  'Is there anything I can do to help?'

- Genuine support, love, kindness and respect – with regular reassurances of all these – can make a huge difference; beliefs due to low self-esteem that no-one cares can be very destructive.

- Express positive thoughts and comments as often as possible:
  'Thanks for … I like it when…'

- Phrase comments on negative eating disorder behaviours in non-judgemental tones. Sandwich such comments between positive messages to show that it is the behaviour you dislike, you still love the person:
  'I love you – and I feel upset when you … I don't like it when you…. I love you so much and am very concerned about what has happened to you and the changes in your life.'
  'I really appreciate how hard you are trying to fight your illness – I find it very difficult to cope when the illness gets strong and you forget about healthy eating again. I love you so much and can see how hard you're trying to beat your eating disorder.'
  This strategy has been called 'the crap sandwich'! – sandwich the difficult bits in between two positives. Use your own words to fit the circumstances.

- Be patient – it is difficult to change and takes time.

4 Try

 Ready to give it a try? What do you expect to happen? What have you learned? Any surprises?

5 If you fail this time

> 'I can't get through to him. He denies everything.'
>
> 'She just got so angry, saying I was being overprotective and imagining things.'
>
> 'She said that she was just having to work hard for exams. She said she was fine though.'
>
> 'Somehow we ended up talking about me! That really wasn't the point!'

Don't consider giving up if your first – and maybe many more subsequent – attempts are met with anger, are ridiculed, ignored, denied or brushed aside.

Don't give up. Keep watching. Wait for other opportunities. The going is very tough – don't give up. Remember during this stage – Edi needs you, but is not yet at the stage to realise it.

6 Other support?

This early stage is very difficult. You may feel lost, alone and confused. You may not be able to get to the stage where Edi agrees that he or she wants help, but in the meantime you can do more awareness and preparatory work.

TAKE ACTION/TRY IT

For example, you could go to your general practitioner yourself, describe what you and other family members observe – notes of incidents and frequency of behaviour can be useful here.

Eating disorders are relatively rare; it may not be an area your GP knows a lot about, s/he may know what text books say but have no knowledge of possible difficulties in the home situation. However, you can ask what help and resources are available in your local area, or where you can find out.

- Concerns about confidentiality: professionals are unable to give you individualised information but they are able to describe the problem in general. Going to your GP, even without Edi, may be a good first step.

- If you find yourself becoming frequently frustrated with Edi, seek support. For instance, Beat runs an eating disorders helpline with volunteers who have had personal experience of an eating disorder in the family. It may be worth speaking to someone who can empathise, and perhaps be able to suggest where to find more relevant information or offer a contact number for a self-help group within travelling distance of where you live.

REFLECTION POINTS

1. Is this an eating disorder? AWARENESS – watch for signs.

2. REMEMBER: getting an individual to accept they have a problem is key – but never easy.

3. PREPARE yourself to broach the subject. Gather information, research and, if possible, talk to others. Decide on a time and place.

4. SCRIPT in your head what you want to say. Rehearse the conversation.

5. TRY IT and TRY IT AGAIN: don't give up. Your concern may initially fall on deaf ears.

6. REFLECT on what you have learnt or skills you have gained.

7. Seek SUPPORT – family/friends? Telephone helpline? Self-help group? Professional? You don't have to survive this alone.

5

Caring styles of close others

It is often very easy for close others to identify the profound ways in which eating disorder symptoms negatively influence a loved one's social, emotional and physical health. Seeing these negative impacts in Edi's life may invoke feelings of fear, anger, frustration and confusion, in addition to other emotions.

The way individual family members respond to the highly stressful circumstances is unique; however, in our experience, there are several common patterns of behaviour that many carers exhibit. These responses, described here using a series of animal metaphors, are *natural* and *typical* reactions to eating disorder symptoms. These are *instinctive* reactions in a concerned and frightened carer. Even when stemming from the best intentions, some of these reactions can have a detrimental impact on the way close others provide help.

Two sets of animal metaphors are used to illustrate common *behavioural* reactions and *emotional* reactions that carers may exhibit in reaction to eating disorder symptoms. See if you are able to notice yourself in any of these metaphors. We hope that *recognising* yourself in the animal metaphors depicted may ultimately improve your rapport and connection with Edi.

> *A look ahead: Chapter 9 goes on to explain how to put these traits to a more productive and beneficial use.*

How do you react? Emotionally

The Ostrich

Some family members may find it difficult to cope with the distress and upset of challenging or confronting eating disorder behaviours. They try to avoid thinking or talking about the problems at all – the 'Ostrich Approach', with head firmly in the sand! While trying to ignore and deny the effects of Edi's behaviour, Ostrich may – or may not – be well aware of consequences for the family. Ostrich may spend as much time away from the home situation as possible, working, constantly

FIGURE 5.1 'Ostrich style' parenting signals that the carer is too busy and unavailable for support. The downside is Edi feels isolated and lonely.

absorbed in programmes on TV or finding any other activity rather than confronting the difficult situation and behaviour of Edi. They may ignore Edi's behaviours and symptoms, and/or undermine the severity of the situation.

Sometimes carers can be engulfed in an intense and transparent emotional response to the illness that is confounded by false interpretations of the illness (see Chapter 2 for myths and beliefs). One common misbelief is that having a child with an eating disorder means they have failed as a parent. High levels of self-blame produce a 'Jellyfish Response'.

Alternatively you may be a perfectionist in your parenting skills and expectations, and hold yourself totally responsible for your child's life and happiness. This sensitive, often tearful, Jellyfish reaction may additionally be due to exhaustion and despair. When carers feel helpless and have this reaction, their own health is affected. Comfort, advice and support may be needed to prevent depression and a further deterioration in the situation.

FIGURE 5.2 Edi elicits a range of intense 'Jellyfish' emotional reactions in the carer. The downside is that the emotional reactions escalate.

The St Bernard dog

We recommend trying to model your emotional response on a St Bernard dog. A St Bernard is calm and collected – even when situations are dangerous. He does not panic or shout and scream, which may cause an avalanche. He is organised, and provides companionship, warmth and nurture. He is dedicated to the welfare and safety of those who are helplessly lost. Calm, warm, nurturing – try to model yourself on a St Bernard.

How do you react? Behaviour

Kangaroo care

'Kangaroo Care' reaction emerges when Edi's fragile physical state draws you in to protect him or her completely, to keep them safe, as if in a pouch. Kangaroo will do everything possible to support and protect Edi by taking over all sorts of aspects of life. Kangaroo will treat Edi with 'kid gloves' in an effort to avoid any possible upset or stress. Kangaroo will accommodate to all demands, whether they are rational or driven by the eating disorder.

- Where binge eating exists, Kangaroo might shop for much larger amounts of food to replace missing food.

- Where undereating exists, Kangaroo might drive miles to find a special food which just *might* tempt Edi's appetite.

- Kangaroo might make special meals just for Edi, which are separate from the rest of the family.

- Kangaroo may rearrange the family schedule to fit Edi's exercise schedule.

The downside of taking over all Edi's responsibilities is that Edi will fail to learn how to approach, cope with and master the challenges of life – and become trapped in the role of an infant.

FIGURE 5.3 'Kangaroo style' parenting means a tendency to overprotect, in this case, to try to constantly keep Edi in a safe place, protected from all difficulty. It is often a carer's own anxiety that leads to strategies to protect Edi from each raindrop. The downside is that Edi does not learn about the realities of the world.

The Rhinoceros response

As a carer, you may become stressed and exhausted by Edi's unremitting intransigence in the face of the, apparently, simple solution – to eat a nutritious and adequate amount – and you may get drawn into adopting a 'Rhinoceros Response' (see Figure 5.4). In addition, tempers may become short as food disappears, the bathroom is in constant use, sinks and toilets are blocked or family meals are continually interrupted. Your temperament may be one that focuses on detail, and so you want Edi to understand your analysis of the situation. Rhino attempts to persuade and convince Edi to change by argument, as if charging at and trying to smash the eating-disordered behaviour and beliefs using logic.

The downside of this is that, if Edi obeys, Edi's confidence in the belief that they can do this themselves, without assistance, will not be developed. Or, as is more likely, Edi may spend all energies in self-protection, arguing back with eating disorder logic, rehearsing all the distorted eating-disordered thinking – and digging a deeper hole to hide in.

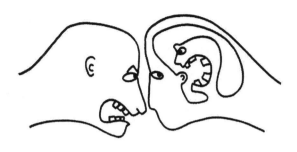

FIGURE 5.4 Eating disorder behaviours can elicit a 'Rhino Response', where you are drawn into a face-to-face showdown to argue the point logically. The downside of this is that gives air time to the anorexic bully, which can help it stick ever tighter.

The Terrier response

The Jack Russell Terrier Response is yapping at Edi's ankles – reminding and quizzing her/him about food and eating. Does this work for you? Or do you think Edi just tunes you out as part of the 'noise' of critical comments and food thoughts that jangle inside his or her head?

Time spent listening to Edi – rather than talking at Edi – is worth its weight in gold.

The Eating Disorder Martyr: Accommodating and enabling

A frequent caregiving response to someone who is ill is to spoil them and treat them as special. Trying not to provoke distress and aiming to keep the peace around someone with an eating disorder may mean accepting eating disorder rules. This involves changing food-related behaviour in the shops, kitchen and dining room – or allowing compensatory behaviours to intrude into family life. This understandable reaction has a bad side effect – it allows eating disorder habits to become even more deeply embedded.

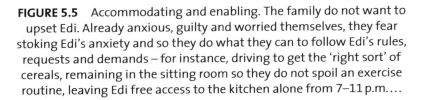

FIGURE 5.5 Accommodating and enabling. The family do not want to upset Edi. Already anxious, guilty and worried themselves, they fear stoking Edi's anxiety and so they do what they can to follow Edi's rules, requests and demands – for instance, driving to get the 'right sort' of cereals, remaining in the sitting room so they do not spoil an exercise routine, leaving Edi free access to the kitchen alone from 7–11 p.m.…

The eating disorder breeding ground

Maybe others in the social network have shared values with Edi (over-emphasising the importance of weight and shape). This may be experienced outside the family – in particular, social media, peers at school or work, sport/dance coaches etc. – but often someone else in the family may have had an eating disorder and has these residual traits. Edi will always try and swing conversations round to food, weight, shape, body image topics. Such conversations give the eating disorder 'air time', strengthening beliefs and habits and propagating more rigid thinking.

caring styles of close others

FIGURE 5.6 Shared eating disorder attitudes. Fat talk rules such as dieting, the over-valuing of thinness and dieting may dominate within the social network.

The Dolphin

Each of the caring styles can offer certain strengths when used as part of a collaborative and integrated approach to helping Edi.

Continuing the animal metaphor, we suggest that rather than falling into Rhinoceros or Kangaroo extremes, try to model yourself on a Dolphin, nudging Edi towards safety. The figure wearing a life vest in Figure 5.7 represents Edi. It is as if Edi is at sea, with the eating disorder as their life belt, unwilling to give up their perceived safety of the life belt whilst they feel that the world is stressful and dangerous. Dolphin may at times swim ahead, leading the way and guiding Edi through difficult passages, at other times swim alongside coaching and giving encouragement and support. And at times when Edi is making positive progress, quietly swim behind.

Perhaps you can recognise some unhelpful features in your own efforts to care for Edi?

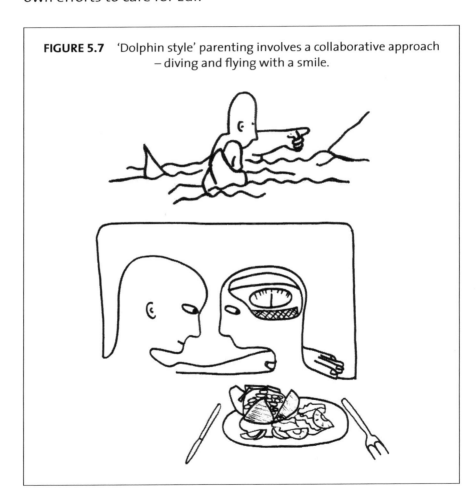

FIGURE 5.7 'Dolphin style' parenting involves a collaborative approach – diving and flying with a smile.

One of the first things that you can do to bring about change in Edi, is to examine and if necessary change your own behaviour. This means stepping back from the unhelpful automatic reactions of, for example, Ostrich, Rhino, Jellyfish or Kangaroo.

As we mentioned in the Preface, this is a 'three for one'; not only do you break a toxic pattern of interaction but also you learn by experience how difficult it is to change – and you show by example that you are ready to make changes. Go through the circular APT steps we outlined in the Preface: AWARENESS, PLANNING, TRYING IT OUT.

 ## Awareness: What kind of carers are other members of the family?

It is common for members of the family to have different styles. More often than not the eating disorder causes splits within the family – those who are 'soft', who give in to Edi's demands and disordered eating habits and behaviours – and those who are tougher. The eating disorder thrives on this division.

FIGURE 5.8 Divide and rule. Individual family members are set against each other (e.g. Dad is perceived by Mum as too soft, and vice versa). So much energy is lost squabbling between family members that the eating disorder wins the day. (These splits can also occur between a treatment team and the family!)

caring styles of close others

Planning for collaboration and cooperation

We cannot stress strongly enough the importance of healing these splits and having a coherent team response. Here is one way you could set about doing this – you will probably think of others; sometimes someone from outside the close family, who can be more detached, can help. (The instructions for this task are given for parents; however, this may need to include other family members – for instance, siblings.)

First, plan to communicate with respect and humour. Set aside uninterrupted time to do it – possibly out for a meal or coffee?

Get two sheets of paper, one sheet for you and one for your partner, and draw four scaled lines on them – two lines which scale emotional reactivity and two for emotional behaviours (see Figure 5.9 at the end of the chapter). Anchor each end with the animal.

Next, on your own sheet, give yourself a mark and also mark your partner on these rulers. Then get together and explain why you gave these marks. Do this in a compassionate, non-blaming way. How similar were the two marks for each person? After discussion, do you want to move the position of the mark?

Ask each other how you can help each of you get into a similar, united position – the consistent 'sweet spot' may be around zero for many behaviours but for eating you both may need to agree on taking a firm line. A step-at-a-time wise approach to goal-setting is needed, done with warmth and compassion.

A Look Ahead

Read some of the later chapters to decide what skills are needed, and where the sweet spot of a consistent caring style needs to be:

Chapter 9: Gives more detail about developing a consistent and supportive caring style.
Chapter 10: A particular emphasis on the challenges for siblings and partners.
Chapter 11. How to manage emotions.

The subsequent chapters focus on the specific skills needed for severe restriction (Chapter 12), binge eating (Chapter 13) and other 'safety' behaviours (Chapter 14) – i.e. those habits that keep the eating disorder stuck.
Once you have done this, you will be ready to TRY IT, and TRY IT again.

Think about which metaphor depicts *your attitudes or behaviour* and those of other members of the family and caring team.

1. Kangaroo? Overprotective, too accommodating and too controlling.

2. Rhinoceros? Angry and forceful, rushing in to make things change.

3. Terrier? Critical and nagging.

4. The Martyr? Accommodating and enabling.

5. Dolphin? Guiding, coaching, encouraging and subtle.

Think who depicts *your emotions*.

1. Ostrich? Preferring escapism and avoidance.

2. Jellyfish? Over-emotional and sensitive.

3. St Bernard? Calm, warm and nurturing.

And finally look at the bigger picture of the environment – are there triggers that keep Edi's thoughts about nutrition in action?

Remember – changing someone else is hard. Changing yourself might be a little easier. Working as a team is essential.

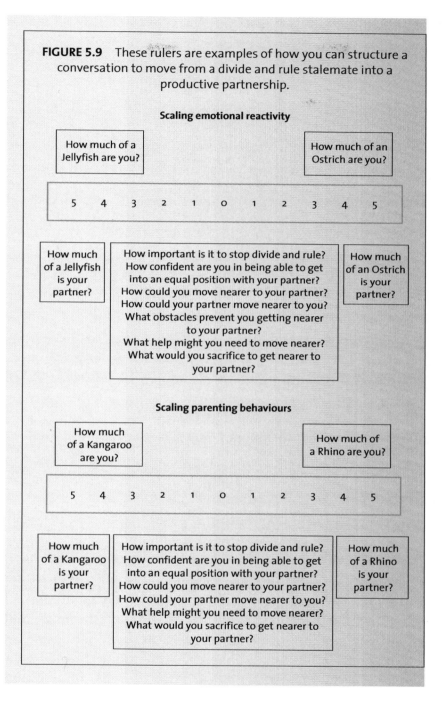

FIGURE 5.9 These rulers are examples of how you can structure a conversation to move from a divide and rule stalemate into a productive partnership.

Scaling emotional reactivity

How much of a Jellyfish are you?

How much of an Ostrich are you?

| 5 | 4 | 3 | 2 | 1 | 0 | 1 | 2 | 3 | 4 | 5 |

How much of a Jellyfish is your partner?

How important is it to stop divide and rule?
How confident are you in being able to get into an equal position with your partner?
How could you move nearer to your partner?
How could your partner move nearer to you?
What obstacles prevent you getting nearer to your partner?
What help might you need to move nearer?
What would you sacrifice to get nearer to your partner?

How much of an Ostrich is your partner?

Scaling parenting behaviours

How much of a Kangaroo are you?

How much of a Rhino are you?

| 5 | 4 | 3 | 2 | 1 | 0 | 1 | 2 | 3 | 4 | 5 |

How much of a Kangaroo is your partner?

How important is it to stop divide and rule?
How confident are you in being able to get into an equal position with your partner?
How could you move nearer to your partner?
How could your partner move nearer to you?
What help might you need to move nearer?
What would you sacrifice to get nearer to your partner?

How much of a Rhino is your partner?

6

Stress, strain and developing resilience

Stress: Why are carers susceptible?

In daily life, a certain degree of stress can serve as a challenge, but – if we can eventually master the problem – it can be energising and fulfilling. However, unrelenting stress beyond our capacity to cope turns into great strain and leads to distress. Living with an eating disorder is a huge challenge, even to a large team of highly trained professionals, let alone any individual family or to a single home carer struggling to support a loved one.

One of the difficulties is that the problem is multi-faceted and affects all areas of life for everyone who shares accommodation with Edi.

The eating disorder's strength can pose a significant threat to any carer's resilience. Once there is a collapse of coping resources, family (or 'home team') members can become depressed or over-anxious, or walk away from the problems, all of which will impact on Edi and their care. Tension between being drawn in to protect and try to help Edi, and frequent rejection (both active and passive) of that help, leads to further misery.

Coping and resilience can be improved through getting the right information at the right time, by learning new skills and building on existing ones. This applies to anyone in close proximity to the sufferer, whether family or friend. The closeness of the relation-ship and amount of time spent together are major factors in how draining on resources the experience can be. In specialist units treating eating disorders, staff burnout, sickness or difficulties with recruitment and staff continuity frequently occur. And in a home situation, individual members may become exhausted and isolated and develop clinical levels of depression or anxiety.

The following text gives you more in-depth information about each of these problem areas.

1 Unwillingness to accept help

If there is a huge divergence between your understanding of the eating disorder and its consequences and that of Edi's, it can cause much friction. In anorexia, carers see that Edi is ill and physically frail, whereas it is Edi's strongly held belief that his or her current weight and physical state are satisfactory. In Edi's view, nothing is wrong. Sufferers of bulimia are also sceptical of the medical consequences of their behaviour. They may feel incapable or unable to conceive their life without the 'release' or coping strategy that purging gives them. It is thus very difficult to persuade Edi to seek medical help – and even more difficult for Edi to adhere to any advice given. This is intensely frustrating for all carers, as it is for professionals. Chapter 7 deals extensively with the prospect of change.

2 Contact time

Often families, determined to do their best for Edi, will be totally committed in their efforts to help and try to be with Edi as much as possible. Unfortunately this superhuman effort can be coun-terproductive, leading to exhaustion and a build-up of tension that may explode unexpectedly or come out in other more subtle ways. Carers have told us that they find that one of the important things in helping their loved one is to start to take some time off; to step back, to reflect and have respite from their caring duties.

Caring for yourself is of vital importance as a core skill in managing eating disorders, enabling you to maintain a calm, compassionate stance. *This is impossible unless you can nurture and replenish yourself.* Not only is this important for your own wellbeing – it also sets an example for Edi of good self-care.

3 Role strain – fostering consistency at home with family and other carers

Within families (and also within professional teams) there are often heated differences of opinion and polarised, conflicting strategies about the role and responsibilities that each family member should take in relation to the eating disorder. This inevitably causes conflict and distress and an inconsistent reaction to the illness. *Consistency* is a core skill and so needs special attention. Husbands, siblings, grandparents and other family members may feel neglected and resent – either passively or by active protest – the attention devoted to Edi.

FIGURE 6.1   The eating disorder uses the gaming tactic of divide and rule. Thus individual family members are set against each other (e.g. Dad is perceived by Mum as too soft and vice versa). So much energy is lost squabbling between family members that the eating disorder wins the day.

Try not to let the illness take over your life entirely. Find time and energy for other family members and their activities, and, as emphasised here, for yourself. This is not easy with such a demanding illness, which affects so many aspects of life. It may be necessary to simplify life in some way, perhaps by explaining how tired you feel and asking for help and delegating, or perhaps by finding at least one role you can drop or share.

> **Try It!** Draw up a list of household tasks, find a time when everyone in your household is together and say you'd like help from everyone who lives in the house. Talk about building a team of helpers. Ask which tasks each person will undertake. *'Would you like to do the vacuuming every week? Help wash the dishes after our evening meal? Or maybe you'd prefer to clean the bathroom? Or…'* In the rush to avoid the tasks people really detest doing, there could be a stampede of offers of help with other tasks they'd prefer. If not, delegate the tasks on your list. And say that the situation can be reviewed after … (set a time, perhaps a review after a week or a fortnight).

APT can be very helpful here too – being aware of how all your efforts to provide the much-needed extra support for Edi is affecting life at home for everyone in the family, including or perhaps especially impact on the main carer. Adapt the ideas in this book to suit your own situation.

The main carer in a household is the person who organises most household chores, cleaning, shopping, cooking, washing and drying the dishes, etc. – for instance, a parent, a sibling, one of a group of flatmates. *Whatever* tasks members of the 'home team' undertake, it is at least lightening the load a bit for the main carer.

First step – raise AWARENESS in the household of how you're feeling, talk about how much energy it takes to, for example, organise the household (cleaning, cooking, shopping…).

Next – PLANNING and TRY IT (see box).

Any changes needed? *Reflect and review* as necessary.

Remember to notice and praise all the new efforts and the increased help being offered.

4 Disorder-related problems

Although meals are the major focus and cause many problems, other symptoms – depression, anxieties, explosive anger, compulsions and rituals, excessive exercise, vomiting, social isolation, to name a few – intrude into family life and are very difficult to manage. It is best if families can work together to plan some time to share and explore ideas and strategies about managing symptoms. Chapters 12, 13 and 14 focus on different approaches to help you, and Edi, problem solve and cope with challenging behaviours.

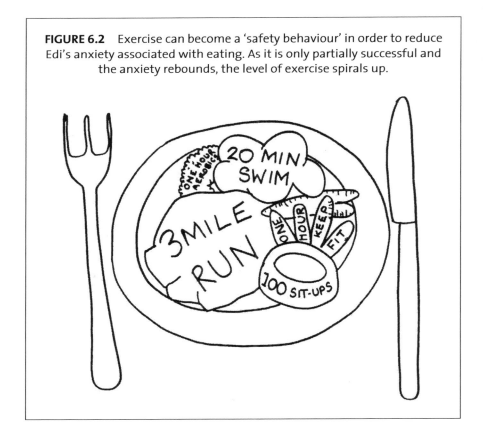

FIGURE 6.2 Exercise can become a 'safety behaviour' in order to reduce Edi's anxiety associated with eating. As it is only partially successful and the anxiety rebounds, the level of exercise spirals up.

5 Beliefs about the illness

In Chapter 2, we discussed some of the common assumptions and myths held about eating disorders. These false beliefs can be harmful as they trigger emotional responses which can get in the way of being calm, consistent and compassionate, and can fuel some of the less-than-helpful personal interactions.

It is possible to alter how aroused and stressed you are by altering how you think about an event. This is the basis of a very successful form of treatment: cognitive behavioural therapy, or CBT. Consider the following example:

> You cannot get to sleep, you are on holiday in a town where a festival is happening and there is noise outside of people laughing, talking and dancing. If you allow your thoughts to be dominated by the idea that people are being inconsiderate, rude and deliberately trying to upset you, it is likely that you will continue to toss and turn as you become more and more angry. On the other hand, if you try to take a different perspective – ask yourself whether the intentions of the others are basically on the side of good. Yes, they are enjoying the pleasures of social connection and contributing to fun and happiness … try to focus on a time when you too enjoyed these pleasures. You may now find that your feelings about the noise can change from anger to pleasure and compassion. The sensation of arousal and being wound up also settles and you can relax. This can allow your behaviour to change from lying tired and restless to peaceful sleep.

In the context of caring for someone with an eating disorder, you may have a preconceived idea that their illness is a wilful act of selfish, attention-seeking behaviour. You may begin to resent Edi – they create family arguments, tension and stress and require much attention and nurture. They are stubborn, obstinate, rude and unpredictable and, without thinking of possible consequences, go against all your advice.

However, informing yourself of the nature of their illness changes your thinking. You read about the subject and discover Edi is medically unwell; their behaviour is unintentional. Your behaviour towards them changes – you have sympathy, show understanding and begin to develop a good rapport with them.

6 Interpersonal relationships

The animal metaphors described in Chapter 5 are a useful adjunct to help identify problematic relationships. Chapter 9 goes on to explain the effect these instinctive reactions have on Edi but the following paragraphs serve as an introduction.

Strategies helpful in eating disorders differ from those that work for an acute illness without any emotional underpinnings. For instance, it is very unlikely to be effective if you try to argue against Edi's eating behaviour, to dominate and demand change (the 'Rhino response'). Indeed, this will probably make the situation worse. In order to help someone overcome their eating disorder, listening to and trying to understand their point of view is essential. Even if you can't understand how or why the individual is thinking and behaving the way they are, you can try to accept that this is how the sufferer feels at that moment.

The emotional tone may oscillate between and within 'home team' members – who may be parents, siblings, grandparents, spouses, children, flatmates, close friends struggling to cope in the outside world with work and other activities while also trying to support Edi, often with little information or help. Unfortunately the extreme responses described – Kangaroo, Rhino, Jellyfish or Ostrich – though natural, can be harmful as they can result in rebellion or regression and even more entrenched eating disorder behaviours. Finding the correct balance of compassionate guidance within a warm relationship, whilst acknowledging the problems caused by the extremely challenging behaviour of the illness, is very difficult.

Remember the need for consistency which can be blown away by strong emotions. In the mantra of the carer, remember the three important Cs – *Calm, Consistent, Compassionate.*

- Beware of 'charging in for change', like a Rhinoceros.

- Beware of trying to provide total protection, by trying to protect Edi in a Kangaroo's 'pouch'.

- Beware of having your emotional responses on display like a Jellyfish.

- Beware of rushing in like a Terrier, constantly yapping on about what you think is needed.

- Ignoring symptoms, hoping Edi will grow out of it, like an Ostrich with its head in the sand, will not help either.

- Beware of striving too hard for peace and changing your life completely to accommodate the eating disorder symptoms.

- Try, instead, to get alongside Edi and help guide in the right direction, rather like a Dolphin travelling alongside and helping to pilot a boat through stormy seas.

- Think of yourself as a St Bernard rescue dog, calmly tracking out to provide warmth and nurture to Edi, lost in the dangerous frozen wastes of an eating disorder.

7 Unmet needs

(a) Caring for your own needs

It is all too easy for each member of a home team/family to feel overwhelmed by the power of the eating disorder. Families can become very isolated as they turn inwards in the struggle to cope.

Many carers do not feel entitled to take any time off for recharging their own batteries. With symptoms often demanding attention many times a day over long periods and affecting all aspects of home life without remission and respite, this is a heavy load. *Therefore, to avoid burnout and stress-related problems, it is important that carers take time to look after themselves and plan their own survival strategies so that they may continue to support the sufferer effectively.*

In addition to asking/discussing how everyone in the household can help with practical tasks, the most important thing carers can do is timetable some pleasurable activities into each week – meet up with friends, follow a hobby or interest either new or old – and make sure you do things for fun or which give a sense of personal achievement. You need to counterbalance the difficulties by having a store of positive experiences to draw upon.

- Draw up a list of your favourite things. Make time for some of them. This is a 'two for one' deal; not only does it stop your automatic defensive reflexes dominating (Jellyfish, Ostrich), but it models an emotionally intelligent way of being – Dolphin – which is a key message for the person with an eating disorder. Respite for you also has a further benefit for Edi: he or she is learning to cope for short times alone and thus slowly building confidence for the future.

- Take care not to drift into cycles of unhelpful behaviours, e.g. drinking to block out how you feel, or isolating yourself by not seeing friends, or stopping doing outside activities – all of which are very easy to slide into when under pressure.

The pressures of caring may take a very heavy toll. Some carers may benefit from professional counselling themselves or may require a GP's advice with regard to a diagnosis of depression and the need for therapy or prescription medication. 'Family therapy' – joint therapy with Edi and one or more family members – may help progress treatment and provide a forum for discussion. The result may be that all family members, particularly the main carer, feel the benefit of more support.

Try to timetable special time with Edi, such as a short walk, a joint game, a comedy video or perhaps a trip to the shops or cinema, etc., which will help you nurture the positive, rewarding and non-eating-disordered aspects of your relationship; unfortunately it is all too easy to lose sight of this. In other words, another C: *cherish* yourself and your whole family.

Change will not happen overnight. It is important for you to set *gradual* goals in which you *slowly* establish a reduction in the amount – intensity and face-to-face hours – of care you give. Use your APT routine to set this in motion. Review regularly how things are going, what has made a positive difference, what doesn't seem to work and what might work better.

Reviewing progress and giving feedback is an important part of re-establishing a measure of independence for the sufferer. No matter how small the step towards assuming personal respons- ibility, whether in nutritional matters or time without company, justified praise for what has been achieved can be given. Make sure you have some way of keeping a tally of the positives – it is easy to forget. If the goal has proved very difficult, praise can be given for the effort in trying. Progress reviews with professionals are also important, with the option of more intensive care if necessary.

(b) Caring for the rest of the family

It is difficult to find enough time for other family members, who can easily feel neglected. Also, your own stress may spill over into your interactions with them and you may sound more irritable and impatient.

Siblings may have developed their own – right or wrong – ideas about the illness and they may have patterns of interaction that are not helpful, e.g. retaliating to irrational anger. Often they blame themselves for not being able to help. They may become angry about their own neglected needs; they may be resentful about feeling obliged to accommodate eating disorder behaviours; they may feel guilty about achieving normal mile- stones. (Some siblings deliberately underachieve in order not to highlight any contrast between their development and that of Edi. Others leave home as soon as they can, and some may even avoid visiting.)

It is important to try to address these issues if they arise. Chil- dren can understand that they may have to wait for time with parents but it is important not to overlook others in the family totally. Draw in other family members to help if you can. Siblings can play an important role by maintaining connections with life outside the eating disorder, such as making a trip to the cinema together, enjoying a walk, a trip to the local swimming pool, a drink out in a café or any other shared activity.

Encouraging everyone in the household to play a part in organising and doing chores can often result in a feeling of 'teamwork' – as well as creating opportunities to talk as they share, e.g. washing the dishes, tidying up and dusting their rooms, discussing what chores need to be done, helping with shopping, helping to make a list for that shopping…

And sometimes the relationship remains difficult. Siblings – and other relations – may be very different sorts of people and may need to accept that they can never 'get it' with each other.

8 Stigma

Many psychiatric disorders are stigmatised by society, possibly in part because these difficulties are hard to understand and people are frightened by what they don't understand. As discussed earlier, the myth that eating problems are caused by the parents can shape your interactions with other people. Feelings of shame and blame can be particularly difficult to bear, and feelings of isolation may follow. However, avoiding friends and other people, on the assumption that they will also blame you and believe in the stigma associated with mental health problems may give credence to the idea that it might indeed be the parents' fault.

Most friends are willing to help when a problem is shared. By never mentioning a problem, the opportunity of offering help and support is denied to those who possibly could and would help. Sharing valuable 'time-out' activities, such as chatting over a cup of tea, lunch out or cooking for a friend, all of which provide respite for carers, also provides ideal times to be heard and listened to.

Remember

There is no magic recipe that works in all cases. Rather, recovery is often a protracted, evolving process with you as a guide or coach.

Carers (both lay and professional) need to be open, to respect each other and to aim to work in synchrony – much easier said than done because the eating disorder often produces strong differences of opinion among carers – divide and rule are the operating principles of this 'minx' who has taken over your loved one. A consistent approach is essential; otherwise the Edi minx will do his or her best to take over your home.

Words by Venables, who had a clinic at Guy's Hospital where he cared for many cases of anorexia nervosa a hundred years ago, are still pertinent now:

> *No patient should remain uncured and no patient should be allowed to die. The doctor (carer) must never admit defeat and never lose his temper ... the opportunities for annoyance will be many.*[1]

Patience and calmness – not common virtues in our striving western societies – are some of the key skills to help with this illness. In the face of the many 'opportunities for annoyance' noted by Venables, they may be hard to develop. Friends and family, a self-help group or spiritual help can all provide important support. Understanding the science underpinning psychological principles can also help construct an environment in which the eating disorder does not flourish.

> *Working together slowly but surely, calmly and consistently, brings positive results – though not overnight.*

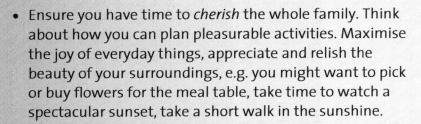

ACTION POINTS

- Ensure you have time to *cherish* the whole family. Think about how you can plan pleasurable activities. Maximise the joy of everyday things, appreciate and relish the beauty of your surroundings, e.g. you might want to pick or buy flowers for the meal table, take time to watch a spectacular sunset, take a short walk in the sunshine.

- Maintain as many links with people outside the family as possible. *Cherish* your social network. *Communicate* with others.

- Spend time with Edi to 'rekindle' and encourage their 'well side'.

REFLECTION POINTS

1. Actively planning strategies to ensure that you can master the elements needed in your role as a caregiver is extremely important to enable and ensure effective caring.

2. This can be a 'two for one' deal – not only will you lessen the strain of the caregiving role, the indirect effect is the opportunity to model for Edi how to master difficulties by self-care.

3. Remember the key Cs to the whole process – Calmness, Compassion, Consistency, Cherishing, Communication and making and maintaining Connections.

Reference list

1. Venables, J. F. *Guy's Hospital Report 80*, 213–222. 1–1–1930.

stress, strain and developing resilience

7

Understanding change

Introduction

Changing *any* behaviour is usually not a simple switch between two options: *'Most days I do this – but tomorrow I'm going to change completely and do this instead.'* There are usually many steps in between depending upon our circumstances, the environment, other people's demands, what we see as the pros and cons of changing and whether we feel confident that we can accomplish change. People do not respond well to being forced to change; however, change is more appealing if it leads to better connections to others.

There are several psychological models that describe how people change their behaviour. In this section, we discuss what is known in theory about change, especially relating to major life-affecting decisions. Addictive and compulsive behaviours can be particularly difficult to change, as adaptations and anomalies in automatic brain processes can obscure the underlying issues.

Stages of change

Changing any behaviour that gets stuck is a complex process. One way to think about it is to divide it into stages and then to think about what is behind each stage and what has to happen to move from one stage to another. A commonly used model that has been used in psychology has five stages.

- Stage 1: *Precontemplation*. This is the stage where the person resists any idea about change and sees no need for change, despite the concern expressed by family and friends.

  - In this situation, Edi has only one mindset – their eating disorder seems to be a solution, offering rewards without any perceived costs.

- Stage 2: *Contemplation*. The person is 'in two minds' about the need to change: juggling thoughts about the pros and cons of change begins, and whether there is enough confidence to do it.

  - In this stage, Edi has two mindsets: (1) seeing the costs and problems that the eating disorder brings, but (2) feeling aware of rewards from their eating disorder, and aware of the obstacles to change. Oscillating between these two mindsets causes confusion and distress.

- Stage 3: *Preparation*. Then comes consideration of change with all the difficulties being recognised, and development of personal determination to at least try to change problem behaviour.

  - In this stage, the resolution of the conflict favours moving away from the eating disorder. The costs of remaining with the eating disorder are seen to outweigh the benefits.

- Stage 4: *Action*. The beginning of real change.

  - In this stage, Edi will have made some steps towards getting help or making changes. However, there is often a physical and psychological rebound of all the things that have been suppressed and so progress is stormy.

understanding change

FIGURE 7.1 The stages of recovery. In *Precontemplation*, Edi can see nothing but the golden cage and fails to notice ways to get out. In *Contemplation*, Edi starts to look at the possibility of change. In *Preparation*, Edi starts to grasp at the possibility of becoming free from the eating-disordered behaviour. In *Action*, Edi works on the process of getting out of the cage. In *Maintenance and Recovery*, the cage is left behind.

- Stage 5: *Maintenance* of change is another particular challenge as the triggers and aspects of the old behaviour seen by Edi as positive remain, and there may be many setbacks.

    o In this stage, Edi consolidates and builds on previous progress. However, developing new connections with the world without the eating disorder takes time and effort.

Edi may go through each stage several times before lasting progress is maintained – do not be too discouraged when setbacks occur; this is part of the illness pattern and recovery process. New things are learnt with each setback and restart. Keep going on the strategies and techniques outlined in this book; actively look for the support needed to continue your caring role effectively.

How people move towards change

Now that you have a basic overview about stages of change, it is important to consider when, how and with what support people can move forward.

There are two main principles. People become more ready to change if:

1. *They feel that it is important for them to change*, i.e. the positive benefits for change outweigh the negative aspects of change.

2. *They are confident that they can change.*

Described in this section is the way we can help move people towards change within individual treatment. This may give you ideas on which you can base your home interactions with Edi.

For someone in *Precontemplation*, the work involved is towards helping Edi to think about the importance of change. Edi is asked to think about how the eating disorder fits with their overall beliefs and values about life both in the past and in the present, raising awareness and self-reflection. Help Edi step back from the detailed focus on eating and symptoms, to consider the bigger picture of his or her life story.

- You cannot do it for them. If you strongly state the reasons, it can dig them in deeper. Edi's non-eating disorder part needs to have a voice.

- The more carers can remain calm and consistent (like the St Bernard) in keeping connections going and keeping channels of communication open in this phase, the more successful progress is likely to be towards reaching contemplation of change.

- If frustration at lack of progress threatens to overwhelm, carers may like to take 'time out' – a walk perhaps, or a change of subject, rather than allowing the eating disorder voice to speak. Try again at a later date when a suitable opportunity can be found.

In *Contemplation* we try to make some of the negative aspects of an eating disorder more prominent and obvious, exploring ways in which Edi's perceived positive benefits of an eating disorder can be attained from other means that do not impact so negatively on the quality of Edi's life and his or her family.

- At this stage, working to bolster self-esteem so that the individual is confident that they can make the changes is really important. This is done by showing respect for Edi's ideas and beliefs, then working to shape their ideas towards change by paying attention to those beliefs which will help Edi towards positive change – and ignoring those that may interrupt it. At the same time we show respect for Edi and stress their right to choose for themselves.

- In this phase, Edi's confusion can be cleared a little by connecting with the thoughts, emotions and values that are on the side of positive change and spending more active listening time developing these while also being respectful, non-judgemental and *compassionate*. While acknowledging them as Edi's thoughts and feelings, their thoughts, emotions and values on the side of *no change* should be given as little attention as possible. At the same time, it is important to notice and encourage the positive actions as often as possible. Building awareness comes in these stages of precontemplation and contemplation.

Once there is a *commitment* to change, you can move to the 'planning and try it' aspects of APT. Set up small behavioural experiments which can lead to Edi achieving new goals towards positive change in eating and diet.

- When people are in *Preparation* we try to help them develop a detailed visualisation of positive change goals, with great attention to detail about implementation – talk about the practical planning and *how* the changes might be managed. One of the goals is to be more flexible and to learn how to adjust to a sudden change – for instance, in developing a goal.

Once in *Action*, the interactive learning cycle of APT is complete. When a new challenge has been mastered it is time to review and reflect on what has been achieved.

How cycle of change can become stuck

Eating disorders tend to persist and are difficult to treat. We can use a metaphor of a snowball rolling down a hill to describe how eating disorders change over time. The symptoms get larger and deeper like a snowball and, at the same time, a slippery slide of eating-disordered habits is formed. The eating disorder gets bedded in and rationalised with layers of anxiety and eating disorder rules and serves some sort of function for Edi. At the Maudsley, when we asked our patients to write letters to 'Anorexia, their friend', they wrote that the illness makes them feel safe; it can make them feel special; it can stifle and suppress emotions and yet serve to signal to other people, in an indirect way, that something is wrong.

Brain starvation produces a frozen waste and accentuates any tendency to be inflexible and rigid, over-analytical, seeing only the detail, rather than being able to synthesise the moment into the tapestry of life. The single-minded focus of eating disorders allows compulsive behaviours and rituals to flourish. Such a strategy may be of benefit: to help Edi avoid thinking or dealing with painful issues about themselves, stressful events or their connections within the world and other people – a very powerful illness-maintaining factor indeed.

Families and other carers have an important part to play in helping with this process of change in different settings. Carers maybe need to make changes too – to learn not to jump in to 'fix it', but to stand back, trust and allow Edi to take responsibility and develop their own skills too. This is essential but difficult for carers, as it will involve watching powerlessly whilst Edi makes mistakes, suffers setbacks and encounters difficulties.

When seeing commitment to change faltering, are you in precontemplation about not rushing in to provide Kangaroo protection? Or possibly tempted again to try the logical argument route favoured by Rhino?

Reflect on your progress through the circle of change. If not successful in the first few attempts, *don't give up*! *Keep calm and allow more time.*

Communicating about change

How you provide support makes a big difference. The illustration in Figure 7.2 depicts the various possible styles of interaction.

FIGURE 7.2 Styles of interaction. The eating disorder can trigger extreme modes of interaction. The top image illustrates avoidance/ignoring (with the danger that Edi is alone with that voice). The image at the bottom illustrates conflict (with the danger that the non-eating part is lost from view). Finding the just-right position, whereby you can elicit conversations with Edi's non-eating-disorder part can be a difficult balance. More information about communication is described next in Chapter 8.

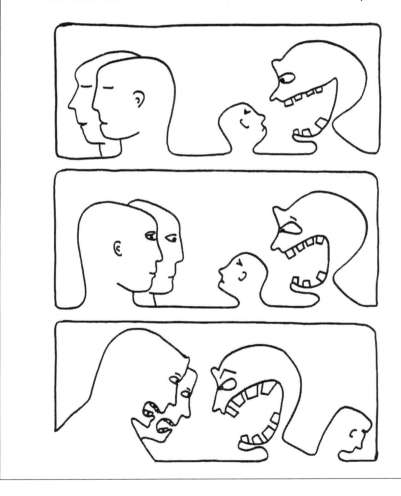

Avoidance/Ignoring style

You may not be willing or able to discuss change with Edi. You may find it unbearable to see how upset she or he gets when you apply *any* sort of pressure, no matter how gentle, and eventually resort to avoiding the issue (like Ostrich). Or it may be that you have your own hang-ups about eating – you may even have had an eating disorder yourself. Consequently, you may find yourself unintentionally colluding with Edi's illness – by being over-accommodating to their behaviour, and over-sympathetic like Kangaroo. Alternatively, the whole situation may become too emotional for you and Edi ends up being a witness to this (Jelly-fish). All these feelings will lead you to have mixed views about discussing change with Edi – *be careful that they do not lead to Edi relentlessly getting deeper into the eating disorder, with pro-longed symptoms.*

Conflict style

Or, like the figure at the bottom of the illustration, you may be determined that Edi will change as soon as possible … it seems a simple solution – just do it, just eat! *The problem with a carer having such drive and determination to generate change is that it can lead into head-to-head conflict with Edi, which may lead to him or her getting even more stuck* (Rhinoceros reaction).

'Goldilocks' style

The ideal position is the one depicted in the middle of the illustration. Think back to the tale of the three bears with Goldilocks finding a middle road in terms of porridge temperature, chair softness and bed size! By being willing to take the time to listen, to try to see Edi's perspective and to go at their pace, you can be determined and persistent in your attempts to help Edi change. Rather than trying to push and shove, you help Edi by gently guiding and motivating towards change (Dolphin).

Work *together*. The aphorism from Beat about change in eating disorders, *'You alone can do it, but you can't do it alone'*, is very true.

Why use the 'readiness ruler'?

The 'Readiness Ruler' is a useful tool that you can use to explore readiness to change and helps you adopt the 'Goldilocks' (Dolphin) position. The Ruler opens the door to change as you can ask questions that focus the discussion on problem solving and solutions. Although it can be helpful to think in terms of stages, it also can be helpful to think of change in terms of a dimension. The 'Readiness Ruler' illustrates this concept:

Measuring readiness to change

Not interested in change   *Eager to put change into place*

0——1——2——3——4——5——6——7——8——9——10

Other advantages to using the Ruler include the following:

- It is a tangible way of reviewing progress – 'That shows you are really moving forward. Fantastic! Two weeks ago, you gave yourself a score of 2 on the Ruler, today you're putting yourself at 4. Please let me know what I can do to help you to keep your thinking at 4 or to move on even further.'

- It is a practical tool with which you both can play, and talk around, avoiding a confrontational approach that can often emerge from eye-to-eye contact.

- The Ruler can be adapted for any behaviour or symptom of eating disorder (see Chapter 12, 'Managing undereating', Chapter 13, 'How to help with bingeing and overeating', and Chapter 14, 'Managing difficult behaviours').

- Although it may seem rather formal, it can help structure a conversation and will stop you falling into any of the Kangaroo, Rhino, Terrier, Jellyfish or Ostrich traps – becoming over-emotional, trying to argue logically against the illogical thinking of the illness, and so on.

- If carers recognise elements of the 'Martyr' or the animal metaphors in their own behaviour, the Readiness Ruler may be a handy way of thinking towards replacing that behaviour and what might better help achieve the positive change.

Is Edi ready to change? Would you place your loved one's readiness to change at the right-hand side of the Readiness Ruler (ready for *Action*?) Or perhaps Edi is in *Precontemplation*, and totally adamant there is no need to change? Or somewhere in the middle?

The readiness ruler is a great tool for collaborative work, either jointly with Edi or with a co-carer

What rating would you give Edi on this line? Then ask your partner/friend also to make a guess. Following this, discuss with each other the reasons that you have given this score. Come up with specific examples of what you have observed to illustrate exactly why you would give this score. Try not to be swayed too much by subjective judgements or what Edi has said; think more about what has been done, and your observations. If you cannot agree at this point, or remain uncertain, plan to review after a period and discuss again.

It can be a source of distress if everyone has highly divergent scores, especially if these are not talked about but simply acted on. The main advantage of using a Readiness Ruler is that the scores are seen overtly. Following discussion about any differences, an agreement can be made to disagree whilst respecting everyone's current perspective, i.e. 'I can see that you are not ready to change *yet*'. (Please note the use of *yet*. It is important to hold an optimistic 'can do' frame of mind, and so temper extreme statements by using modifiers 'yet', 'at the moment', 'with the present perspective', 'currently' – which leaves the door open for a possible change of heart and mind at a later date.)

> *'I understand that it is entirely up to you whether you decide to change or not. However, the illness does affect the family, your relationships with friends and at work, as well as your future, and so I am drawn in.'*

Saying it

People tend to act in a way that is consistent with what *they have said out loud to an audience*. That is why we suggest scripting, visualising and vocalising in PLANNING.

The Readiness Ruler is a useful listening device in opening the way for an exploration of ideas as it can promote 'change talk'; it demonstrates a recognised psychological rule in understanding how people change – that if someone has talked about even the possibility of making a change, it is more likely that they will follow through with action.

A constant complaint of people with eating disorders is that no one listens to them. Indeed, we all often 'tune out' to 'eating disorder talk' as the compulsive aspects – for instance, prolonged descriptions lasting hours, of recipes and their respective merits, or description of a trip to a supermarket, with each item bought described in great detail – are so obviously unhelpful. Also, reinforcing this type of talk by giving it our time and attention is unhelpful.

At the same time, listening and talking about non-eating disorder things, or possibilities of change from the eating disorder behaviour, is essential. Therefore, listening carefully for these more healthy topics interwoven into the unhealthy focus on eating and food – and eliciting and development of even *the possibility* of change to more healthy behaviours – is an important skill for carers to develop.

TABLE 7.1 Small steps to change with the readiness ruler

- Start by asking Edi to give him or herself a score on the Readiness Ruler.

- Talk about both their overall readiness to change – how important is it to them? – and how confident they feel in their abilities to work towards positive change.

- Then open up the conversation by saying, '*I am interested that you have given yourself that score. What makes you give yourself that score rather than, say, 0?*'

- Listen carefully to what is said. Ask what score on the Ruler she or he thinks you might give. Ask her or him why she or he thinks this. Again, listen carefully to the replies.

- Then say what score *you* would give, and state your reasons – your specific observations – why you think this. This will help initiate talk about change.

- Remember: try to steer a conversation so that *Edi* – rather than you – gives the arguments for change. Listen out for *any* change talk and then try to summarise what has been said. A repetition and reflection of change statements will emphasise them.

- Remember: change is more likely when an individual has voiced the desire or need for change.

EXAMPLE:
Edi: '*I have given myself 5 because I know that one of my ambitions is to have a family and I know that it is out of the question at this weight.*'
Carer: '*You're anxious about your future. You are worried that having an eating disorder may have future implications for having a family.*'

Edi's replies reflect clearly the concern the individual experiences (or not). Reflecting on what Edi tells you shows that *you have listened.*

The conversation may then flow on to what would need to happen or what help would be required to get to a higher score.

> 'What do you think might have to happen for you to get a higher score?'

By the end of this exercise, you may have heard some elements of commitment to positive change on which to build. If not, after a period of time calmly try again. Perhaps mention that, '*The doctor/ therapist feels that your nutritional health is at risk ... let's try the Readiness Ruler again. What score do you think you might give yourself now?*' Again follow the Small Steps (Table 7.1) through.

Next steps

> '*Is there any help I can give that would enable you to move nearer to the 10 side of the spectrum?*'

This offer of social support promotes change and can get people thinking positively about help and support towards change – they are not alone in the struggle. Even if a gentle offer of support is initially refused, Edi may think about it and return later to the idea – try to keep all lines of communication open to the possibility of change.

This exercise can be repeated on several occasions and used for many different types of unwelcome behaviours in eating disorders, including obsessive compulsive rituals, vomiting or use of laxatives.

In summary, the aim of the Readiness Ruler exercise is to help your loved one reflect on their eating disorder and how it may affect their life both currently and in the future. This will involve trying to understand the mixed feelings that Edi has about the illness and about change. Many of the positive (perceived by Edi) and negative aspects of an eating disorder are unconscious or inaccessible. It is important to keep listening in order to understand the forces that keep the eating disorder fixed. *Listen* to find where and when there are openings and opportunities for providing further information and help. Grab those moments!

Although remember – it is common for people to go up and down the Readiness Ruler, backwards and forwards through these various stages of change several times.

Carers who want to change

Carers who recognise in themselves behaviour which might be unhelpful – Kangaroo, Rhino, Terrier, Ostrich, Jellyfish – in supporting Edi's struggle with the compulsions, may also find it helpful to use the Readiness Ruler to rate their *own* attitudes to difficult behaviours that affect their lives as well as Edi's. There are several questions to reflect on with your partner or a friend – how *interested* are you for Edi to change? How *important* to you is it that she or he changes as soon as possible? How *confident* do you feel that you can help Edi change? You may want to make guesses about each other's scores and then check with each other how correct you are.

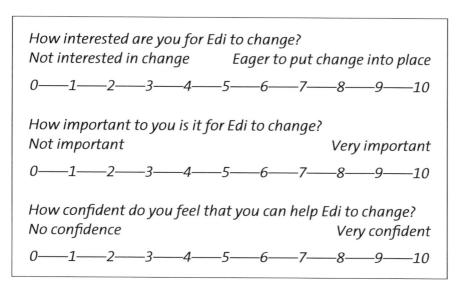

How interested are you for Edi to change?
Not interested in change   Eager to put change into place
0——1——2——3——4——5——6——7——8——9——10

How important to you is it for Edi to change?
Not important   Very important
0——1——2——3——4——5——6——7——8——9——10

How confident do you feel that you can help Edi to change?
No confidence   Very confident
0——1——2——3——4——5——6——7——8——9——10

 **REFLECTION POINTS**

1. Unlike most people who are ill, people with an eating disorder often do not recognise that they have a problem, and do not want to change.

2. Conflict and frustration are lessened if expectations are paced with the readiness to change.

3. The odds of change occurring are increased if Edi is given the opportunity and encouraged to talk about change in him or herself and any concerns they have about being able to change.

4. It is important to have a stance that remains optimistic and firm – and yet is not too pushy for change.

5. The more carers, both home and professional, can be warm, calm and compassionate, the more confidence Edi will gain that she or he can initiate and maintain change.

Again, remember that '*Every mistake is a treasure*' can be helpful in encouragement towards positive effort and change. We all make mistakes, and we can learn from them – and do better next time.

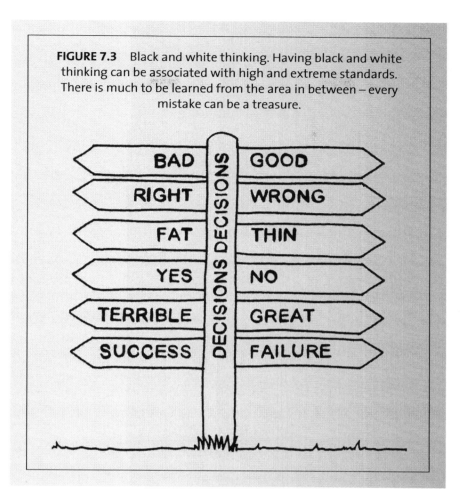

FIGURE 7.3 Black and white thinking. Having black and white thinking can be associated with high and extreme standards. There is much to be learned from the area in between – every mistake can be a treasure.

8

Communication

This chapter is lengthy and deals with the important topic of communication. The beginning of the chapter (pp. 88–94) gives an overview of the communication process and some concise ideas for those who lack confidence in this area. The latter part of the chapter takes you as a carer through different 'communication skills' topics. These skills will further develop your resources to steer Edi, in the long term, towards recovery and health and, in the short term, improve home life, atmosphere and family relationships. Each skill will take time, practice and patience to learn. Do not try to take in everything at once!

How communication happens

In daily life, most conversations are practical exchanges, such as: 'Will you be back for tea tonight?' or 'Where's my blue shirt?' Although tone, context and accompanying body language may indeed positively or negatively influence an existing relationship, most conversations are not particularly planned or designed to develop relationships constructively, and words are often chosen on a functional and perhaps careless basis. However, in addition to the word choice, tone, context and body language of the speaker, the outcome of an interaction is largely determined by the way the words are received. Especially when communicating with someone suffering from an eating disorder, there may be

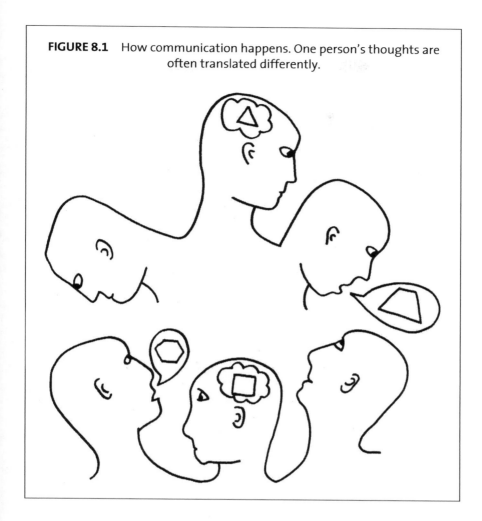

FIGURE 8.1 How communication happens. One person's thoughts are often translated differently.

times when even the most innocuous remark strikes a chord, resulting in an unexpected reaction.

When emotions run high and thinking becomes tunnel-visioned – often the case when living with eating disorders – it is easy for the communication process to go wrong. In such situations, it is even more important to take care and to allocate time to reflect on any inadvertent ruptures and to try to repair damage as soon as possible. As always, every mistake is a treasure – we all make mistakes, and can learn from them.

Some starter points for 'communication beginners'

When family life includes a member suffering from an eating dis-order, communication often becomes fraught. Conversations become derailed because Edi's confidence has reached rock bottom, leading to distorted understanding of what is meant. Where interest is intended, criticism may be assumed; where loving concern is intended, intrusion may be assumed by Edi. Coaching conversations which use a great deal of reflective lis-tening (which will be described further later in the chapter) can help prevent being at cross-purposes in this way.

Building self-confidence

With Edi's very low confidence, carers can act as coaches helping to rebuild self-esteem, fostering the belief that Edi too can be effective in his or her own life. This can be done by helping Edi notice positive aspects of themselves – their abilities and skills, tasks they have successfully completed both currently and in the past. Gradually, by taking every opportunity to increase warmth in the relationships, by 'modelling' or showing by example, you can support Edi towards gradually learning to think better of them-selves. By doing so, you can help Edi develop the effective self-nurturance and emotional intelligence needed to beat the illness.

Of course, it will not be possible to make every conversation deep and meaningful. However, in treating eating disorders, it is particularly important for carers to seek opportunities to actively foster motivation towards changing difficult behaviours affect-ing health and well-being. This will not be a one-off event, but an ongoing process of encouragement on what may be a long road.

Increasing warmth

Communication style is very important in nurturing a healthy social environment. To switch this system on, high levels of warmth, affirmation and calmness are needed, as well as suppression of criticism and irritability. This is a tough task as the eating disorder 'bully' is highly frustrating and so the opportunities to be exasperated are enormous. It is important to bear in mind that people with eating disorders are super-feelers for threat and criticism, so a fleeting loss of mindful communication between you and Edi can have adverse consequences on how Edi feels about him or herself – and lead to an explosion of bad temper. The sound of your voice is very important – using gentle tone is very helpful.

Your facial expression can also make a difference – try to have an open, curious expression with your eyebrows raised, sitting back in your chair. It may be helpful for you to watch a YouTube clip that brilliantly illustrates how differently we interpret raised and lowered eyebrows. Look up 'Talking Eyebrows – Michael McIntyre's Comedy Roadshow' on YouTube.

Here are a few tips for enabling healing conversations:

- voice – tone and volume: soft, gentle, kind

- stance: equal, guiding

- attitude: collaborative, eliciting

- gesture: low power

- eye contact: variable

- eyebrows: raised rather than down

- personal space: side by side, on same level

- expression: interested

- slow to chide and swift to bless with a smile, a hug, a kiss.

Think of VIEW

Notice and comment on the good things that Edi does and give praise for them – use Very Important Encouraging Words (VIEW) wherever possible.

It is helpful to develop your own 'Useful Sentences' to draw attention to progress. This may at first feel a bit awkward, so it is worth practising – perhaps with a friend, or in a mirror – so that they come more and more easily when you need them.

'Thank you for…'

'I noticed that you…'

'I really like it when you…' [name it – help me tidy up, keep your room tidy, bring in the washing, put out the bin – *anything* you can praise, no matter how small]

'I can see you're trying hard.'

'I know how difficult this is for you [name it – e.g. finishing a meal or snack, refraining from visiting the bathroom immediately after a meal, cleaning up after a binge] *and I really appreciate how hard you are trying.'*

Additionally, make special efforts to offer physical displays of love and affection; reach out to show you recognise and value the person, whilst still acknowledging the effects of the eating disorder. Edi may not always respond positively to this praise – especially at first – as it contradicts the loud, negative voice of the 'eating disorder minx' giving their negative self-image.

Keep at it! With time, Edi will get better at accepting and internalising these compliments.

The family's role

Within families we all break the rules about good communication – we may interrupt each other, we may assume we know what another family member's reaction will be without actually discussing the matter. We have such busy lives that we often do not take the time or trouble to really listen to each other. We often assume that we can mind-read or that we know best.

Once you have the problem of an eating disorder in the family it is particularly important and necessary to follow all the rules of good communication. A constant refrain of individuals with an eating disorder is that people do not listen – however, you need to use the *right sort* of listening, and listen to the *right things*.

To cope with all the difficulties an eating disorder can bring, families need to function as a well-run committee! It is helpful to set aside time regularly so all can talk to each other in a *calm, controlled atmosphere* (not during meals). This can be done formally with an agreed time and place free from interruptions, or it may be more informal – for example, making sure that carers are around at a particular time and are relaxed with time to spare, perhaps reading papers on Sunday morning, a short walk to the bus stop or walking the dog together. Can you think of a good time and place for your own family and circumstances?

BOX 8.1 Some ground rules for good communication

1. Only one person speaks at a time.

2. Give Edi the opportunity to talk about change and the bigger picture, with encouragement to talk about life without an eating disorder as much as possible, e.g. *'I'm interested in what you remember of our trip to see …' 'I'd like to hear more about…'*

3. If possible, allow Edi to have the majority of the speaking time away from the eating disorder, especially when the talk is of *change*. Ideally all family members should have an equal time to speak but, as discussed in Chapter 7, positive change is more likely to occur if Edi has the opportunity to talk about any positive changes.

4. At the same time, try to limit the opportunity for the eating disorder voice to talk about eating disorder rules. A few real-life examples:

    'As discussed before, it is not helpful to give airtime to eating disorder talk – let's change the subject. Let's talk

---

about what we'll do when … (e.g. we go to visit Grandma; we want to watch … on TV, but I know Nick would like to watch the boxing; we'll take Rusty for a walk when Uncle Mike is here, where will we go?)'

5. The aim is not to get on a soapbox and deliver a standard script but to work at really understanding what each person is saying.

6. The atmosphere should be *calm, compassionate, warm* and *respectful*.

7. Try to keep the focus on the positive side, i.e. glass half full rather than half empty, by referring to any achievements and progress, no matter how small.

Discuss and agree a maximum time for each contribution to the discussion; perhaps appoint a team member as time keeper (the youngest?), who indicates when individual 'talking time' is up (possibly by ringing a small bell).

Listening

Listening to each other and understanding what the other is saying sounds easy. In fact, it is very difficult and takes skill and practice. If we are listening, we need to *give non-verbal signs* – eye-contact, a nod perhaps or shake of the head, eyebrows raised, a small smile, 'attention sounds', such as *mmm* and *uh-huh* – that we are attending to the speaker. A good way of proving that we are listening is to test whether a *summary or a précis of what we have heard* fits what the speaker means:

- A summary may even just be a simple repetition of what the speaker has said, but it is best if you put it into your own words rather than risk sounding like a tape-recorder.

communication

- A summary of what you think has been said and what you think the speaker meant can be a useful way of clarifying the content.

- Often meanings and understanding of words and concepts can be used idiosyncratically, with meaning dependent on the listener's background, experience, vocabulary and the person's use of that vocabulary, state of alertness or tiredness. *Everyone* has a personal background, which often means individual understating of particular words and phrases – which can sometimes lead to misunderstandings

- In summarising, it does not matter if you do not get it quite right. In some ways it is helpful to get it a bit wrong and mistake the individual's meaning, as that can lead the speaker to add more detail and repeat their thoughts.

The important thing about listening is to show that you are willing to give the time and energy to try to understand. Not only does this signify listening, but it gives the speaker a chance to reflect on what they have said – often we do not know what we think until we say it! Listening carefully, with reflection on what you hear, allows Edi to recognise thoughts, and put them into words. As behaviour change is more likely to follow the expression in words of any thoughts of change, you want Edi to *talk about change as much as possible.*

Getting it wrong: Mistakes and treasures

Here we diverge to discuss another important truism from audit research which is also true about caring for someone with an eating disorder – *'Every mistake is a treasure'.* One of the core vulnerabilities of people with eating disorders is that they are overly concerned about making mistakes, and so they become trapped within a predictable, error-free, eating disorder cage. If, as a carer, you can show that you are not frightened of admitting that you have made a mistake, that you are willing to think about what you have learned from it, and that you can be flexible enough to shift your approach in the light of new learning, then you are transmitting an important life skill.

Involving emotions

Change can be promoted if the emotional tone is gentle, *warm and accepting*. You may be angry towards the eating disorder part of Edi but remember that Edi is much more than merely the eating disorder; Edi still has a non-eating-disorder part too, no matter how deeply buried for the moment. Try hard to focus on the bigger-picture aspects of your loved one as an individual separate from the illness part. Show Edi as much love, care, encouragement and warmth as you possibly can.

Communication skill 1: Motivational interviewing

Motivational interviewing was developed in order to work effectively with people who do not want to change – for instance, in the addiction to drugs or alcohol. You may find reading the textbooks that describe this approach helpful.[1,2,3] The following list of 'Do's and Don'ts' is based on an examination of the interactions from hundreds of therapeutic sessions which form the skills used in motivational interviewing, which is an important part of treatment of eating disorders at the Maudsley Hospital.

Don't

- Argue, lecture or try to persuade with logic.
- Assume an authoritarian or expert role.
- Order, direct, warn or threaten.
- Do most of the talking.
- Make moral statements, criticise, preach or judge.
- Ask a series of (three) questions in a row.
- Tell Edi that they have a problem.
- Prescribe solutions or a certain course of action.

Do

- Let Edi present the arguments for change, and give the opportunity to talk about, and hopefully resolve, ambivalence.

- Focus on your loved one's concerns.

- Emphasise that Edi has the choice and responsibility for deciding their own future behaviour.

- Explore and reflect upon Edi's perception of the situation.

- Reflect what you think you have heard with statements starting with 'You': 'You feel…', 'You think…'.

- Summarise periodically.

- Aim to be as warm and loving as possible.

- Beware of hostility and criticism.

The listening, motivational approach may seem very different from the role you have been used to, leading to feelings of frustration as you have to bite your tongue and not immediately offer your expertise and wisdom, and curb any instincts you have to take over care. (Remember the animal metaphors!) Carers need to allow Edi to have a platform from which to experiment and to express what she or he thinks. The best way for Edi to do this is if there is an outside audience allowing a reflective test-bed of ideas.

'LESS is more' is the spirit of motivational interviewing. *LESS* is the key to this approach:

- L – *Listen*

- E – *Empathy not sympathy*

- S – *Share* non-eating disorder parts of life

- S – *Support*; increase confidence

L – Listen Listening conveys respect for another person's views and emotions. With Edi focused on food and shape, try to tap into the deeper meanings behind that talk – food and shape talk is usually a metaphor for emotional distress or negative beliefs about the self. People with an eating disorder often have quite strong beliefs that they themselves are deeply flawed or unworthy.

Some of the beliefs, thinking and talking about food and shape may cover up:

- *'I hate myself; no one could possibly love me.'*
- *'I'm not worthy of love.'*
- *'Showing feelings is wrong.'*
- *'People will think I'm stupid if I say anything.'*
- *'I'm not good enough.'*
- *'I feel different to other people.'*
- *'I don't belong here.'*
- *'I'm different/weird/a freak.'*
- *'Life is threatening.'*
- *'It's wrong to ask for what I want: I must please others.'*
- *'Everyone is better than I am.'*
- *'Other people are luckier than I am.'*
- *'I must be strong and brave.'*
- *'Being frightened or crying is weak.'*
- *'I must be perfect.'*
- *'I must feel guilty for what I've done.'*

- *'I must not make mistakes or ask for help; that would be failing.'*

- *'It's wrong to have pleasure.'*

- *'I don't trust others.'*

Do not get drawn into a dialogue with Edi about food, weight or shape, but rather say something like, *'It sounds as if you are upset'*. Remember – carers need to demonstrate the skill of being able to step back from detail. Whenever tempted to join in a discussion about food or shape or weight *STOP*, step back, withdraw: *'I can hear you talking to me about eating disorder concerns. It sounds as if you are terrified.'*

In order to show you are really listening, try to avoid letting loose a battery of questions, which often indicates you are attempting to direct the conversation and to be in control. When you are really listening, you will have one or two questions and then encourage the person to talk more and clarify what they are saying by making a précis or summary of what they mean.

E – Empathy Empathy means trying to step into the other person's shoes and to see things from their perspective and to understand their emotional response. Give empathy not sympathy – sympathy implies that Edi is a passive helpless victim. This illness can only be cured when Edi takes an active role; when Edi him or herself develops and practises withstanding the compulsive concerns with courage and stamina.

Following the **C** agenda, it is important to speak with *compassion*, a similar concept to empathy. Only Edi can decide when and how to change. Some parents have difficulty tolerating distress in their children and in doing so can inadvertently invalidate their child's emotional pain, by saying something like, *'That is rubbish! Look at how clever and pretty you are – you can't mean that you are worthless!'* The irony of such a statement is that it emphasises how the person and their thoughts and feelings are discounted and rejected.

It is important for you to try to validate Edi's feelings, experience and perceptions by thinking of the eating disorder as an illness of the emotions. Rather than trying to argue logically with the eating-disordered thinking, try to coach in more emotional intelligence, i.e. for Edi to have that experience and to feel the pain of it but to have the courage to work through it. Rather than withdraw and avoid that experience and the associated pain, help Edi to keep trying to connect, perhaps with a changed goal,

S – Sharing and Support   A warm, loving, supportive atmosphere is the key to overcoming an eating disorder, but is often difficult to achieve given the hostility and rejection Edi displays towards anyone close who spends time in his or her company. (Carers may find it helpful to remind themselves that Edi is expressing and projecting unhappy feelings about the world in general – and you unfortunately happen to be standing in the firing line!)

Share in non-eating disorder behaviours and activities, perhaps a hobby, such as a jigsaw (maybe you can have one made from a photograph of happier times), tapestry or painting, puzzles such as crosswords, cards or board games such as Scrabble that you can jointly play and then leave. Maybe have a book or poetry club? Or copy radio panel games/ideas such as Just a Minute, The News Quiz, etc. Parents, siblings and other family members, close friends and relations can all have a core role here.

Directive elements in motivational interviewing

In addition to the principles embodied in LESS, motivational interviewing also has some more directive elements, using strategies that help Edi move towards greater readiness to change by creating questions in his or her mind between the status quo – in which the eating disorder forms the individual's identity – and their own deeper ideals, values and ambitions. Chapter 7, 'Understanding change', concentrates on this aspect.

Communication skill 2: Tackling conversation traps

It is all too easy to fall into a reciprocal, reassurance-giving, trap. What do we mean by reassurance traps? Answering questions about shape are common ones: *'I won't get fat, will I?', 'I won't be able to stop eating, will I?', 'You haven't put oil in that casserole, have you?'*

People with an eating disorder have high levels of anxiety and they often look to carers to provide reassurance. The problem with giving Edi constant reassurance is that: (1) the relief from anxiety is only temporary – self-doubt and anxiety soon rage again; (2) Edi does not learn that she or he, the individual, can master fear and doubt, and is locked into a dependent relationship. Edi comes to rely on others to reduce anxiety and to check out thoughts. In this scenario, carers can become locked into providing the pouch (Kangaroo), and the eating disorder symptoms flourish.

It is harmful rather than helpful to have prolonged discussion about the details of food or weight or shape or negativity – this merely adds validity to the ideas. Sidestep this. Here are some suggestions to sidestep food and weight talk:

- *'It sounds as if your eating disorder anxiety is strong.'*
- *'You seem frightened.'*
- *'That is your eating disorder speaking to you.'*
- *'Be brave; it will pass.'*
- *'I have read that if I reassure you it will keep your fear flourishing.'*

- *'If I join in with food or weight talk I will lock you deeper into your eating disorder.'*
- *'I do not enter into discussions about food or calories. We will change the subject.'*
- *'As we have discussed, speaking to the "Eating Disorder" voice is harmful.'*
- *'I will listen to you talk to me for five minutes about food/weight/shape, but that will be it for the day.'*
- *'It sounds as if you might be confused about making changes…'*

Communication skill 3: 'Mind physiotherapy'

 ACTION POINTS

Games and activities that 'tone up' a bigger-picture style of thinking, or physiotherapy for the mind, help focus thinking away from eating disorder concerns. Try, for example, 'What the Papers Say' – extracting through discussion the gist of a newspaper or magazine article that appeals – or card or board games. Discussion of diagrams or images can also be used to structure conversations in a positive direction.

Stepping back to see the bigger picture is helped by practising skills such as constructing sound bites, headlines, text messages. Think up some metaphors. Try to make these into a light-hearted game.

The ability to be adaptable is another aspect of brain function. Introducing 'planned flexibility' through non-eating disorder activities in the family and Edi's life can be a means of bolstering an identity which can embrace change. In your individual family situation, how can a home environment be set up so that there is an opportunity to do things differently? In therapy we suggest that people can challenge themselves by coping with chance, e.g. setting up tasks related to the throw of a dice or opening sealed envelopes – you might be able to try this as a form of family game.

It is better to introduce flexibility into non-food areas of life first, e.g. taking different routes to work at varying times; wearing something different, a hat or scarf; listening to a different TV or radio channel; then try within the food domain. Here are some examples:

Rather than continuing to eat only strawberries for breakfast Jane played a form of 'Simon says' and added whatever her mother was eating that morning.

Rather than eating the same snack in the same time and place, Susan agreed to find something to eat within an hour of snack time, no matter where the family were.

Rather than eating the same snack item, Tom agreed to fill envelopes with seven different options and select one at random each day of the week.

Communication skill 4: Atmosphere

One of the most important elements families can promote is to ensure *a warm atmosphere at home*, with as little criticism and hostility as possible. It is important that any negative comments about eating disorder behaviours and their effect on Edi and other family members be made *calmly and gently*, through *I think* and *I feel that* comments, rather than by direct accusation.

As outlined in Chapter 5, many carers – especially parents – blame themselves, feeling that they have somehow failed to protect their loved one. Unfortunately many older textbooks about eating disorders even encourage this self-recrimination. Guilt and self-blame are unhelpful and inaccurate. Furthermore, they are dangerous concepts as they can lead to anxiety and depression.

The following feelings can often trigger unhelpful emotions:

- *Shame and stigma*: The symptoms of anorexia nervosa are highly visible and clear for everyone to see. They strike at the core of being a parent, which is to nurture your child. Carers may feel guilty and ashamed as if other people may judge them unfairly as uncaring and unable to nurture Edi – in other words, as an inadequate, pathetic parent. To some outside observers, Edi is an overt marker of failure in good parenting. *Try to correct this misconception – there is no one trigger or explanation. Perhaps describe the ideas in this book and suggest the critical observer learn more about eating disorders from reading it? Or even offer a loan of it to read?*

- *Anger*: Carers may think that this is just a passing phase and easy to treat, getting angry and frustrated that treatment is slow and not rapidly effective. When you feel you have always done your best and want only to see your loved one well, there is a natural counter-reaction in response to Edi's frequent and extreme outbursts of anger, hostility and rejection – all part of the illness. *Do not rise to the bait and join in with this symptom – remain calm; rather than risk an escalating confrontation, take time out if and when needed.*

- *Fear*: Carers may be terrified at the physical consequences of the eating disorder. Can Edi's body take the strain? Edi may self-harm in other ways, e.g. by cutting, or taking overdoses. You will fear for Edi's safety. *Accurately assess Edi's medical risk (see Chapter 3). Then, calmly and clearly ask (your GP? or other health professional?) for the resources you need to enable you to manage the situation safely.*

- *Loss*: All the expectations about Edi's future will need to be readjusted. Carers feel devastated about the misery, punishment and deprivation in his or her life, and how the illness affects the whole family. *Work to build and strengthen your relationship on a day-by-day basis. Reassess progress and change on a regular basis – look at the positives, however small.*

Communication skill 5: Emotional intelligence

As a carer you want to provide care and safety; it is not easy to show your love with so many negative emotions around. However, outbursts of intense emotion – anger, misery, frustration, grief, emotional pain – with automatic, non-thought-through emotional responses and gut feelings on the surface, are detrimental to setting the scene for positive change. It is not wrong to have these reactions, but rather it may not be helpful for Edi to see you grappling with these intense, raw feelings. *Raw emotions can be toxic for someone with an eating disorder who is in an emotionally vulnerable state, feeling uncertain and unskilled in this area.*

Ideally carers need to model 'emotional intelligence'. This means being able to reflect on, digest and move on from emotional reactions. In professional situations, this is done by having 'supervision' (or support from someone more experienced, a mentor, and achieving detachment from the situation). For carers, this means having *time to step back and discuss with others what might be happening.*

ACTION POINTS

- It is important to try to process and understand all the strong emotional reactions stirred by an eating disorder within the family. Whenever possible, set up something similar to 'supervision' for yourself with friends, relatives or other carers (if you cannot find a self-help group nearby, perhaps help to start one). Spend time with trusted, wise, close others exploring your feelings, beliefs, attitudes and needs – by sharing problems as well as joys, friends will feel able to do the same in their own troubled times. An alternative is to write down your thoughts about the issues involved, which will enable you to explore your feelings more fully. Your thoughts and writing may be shared with others, or not, at a later date. Keeping a journal can be a good way of recording events, thoughts, feelings and reactions, and may also be useful later in reminding of progress.

- In our work with carers at the Maudsley, we ask people to spend some time writing about what it is like to live with anorexia nervosa, later sharing these essays and reflecting on their meaning. Once these emotions and what they are trying to say are understood, and have been evaluated as to whether they are based on realistic appraisal or not, then decisions can be made about how to act on them. You may find that taking time to write things down will help you understand why, how and in what way you are upset. Once you can reflect on your thoughts as a compassionate observer, who can look from all sides of the argument, you may be able to see better your way forward.

- It is helpful to practise – either alone or with a friend – a few phrases you can have ready for difficult situations which might lead you to behave in an emotionally unintelligent way, e.g. when you feel overwhelmed by a quick and angry response to one of Edi's outbursts. These phrases may be practised with a supportive friend or family member, so that they are there when needed and ready to help you step back and defuse the situation, e.g.:

- *'I don't think this is a good time to discuss the matter. Let's talk about it later when we are both calm.'*

- *'We've both said what we think, now I'm going to…'*

- *'My emotions are too intense to think clearly at the moment. Let's come back to it later.'*

---

communication

Communication skill 6: Making rules and setting boundaries

Because of Edi's strong influence, and the temptation to be a martyr, certain existing family rules may have been disrupted and need to be re-established. In order to cope with the demands of the illness, new, different and/or adapted rules may need to be worked out, agreed and established – for example, not eating all the food so there is nothing left for other family members for breakfast; not occupying the kitchen and excluding others who want to use it; not dictating exactly what is eaten for dinner and how it is prepared/cooked, etc.

How do you set limits when Edi is so obviously ill? Or, when bingeing and purging are so shaming and unpleasant you want to avoid confronting them?

House rules often change when there is illness, any illness, and in particular long-lasting conditions. As an eating disorder is a problem that can last months or even years, you need to have rules that you can stick to for a long time. All family members need boundaries – what kind of behaviours are acceptable/unacceptable? Boundaries need to be set out clearly and consistently; a whole-family round-table discussion of what is and is not acceptable can be really powerful.

Think of the Cs:

- You need to be firm about your expectations, and be *consistent*.
- When discussing rules and expectations, show respect for each other and remain *calm*.
- Note and praise any progress (*cherish*).
- When a rule is broken, remind Edi that you know how difficult it is for him or her to overcome eating problems and you are sure she or he will try hard and win next time (*compassion*).
- Remember – it is the behaviour of the illness you dislike, not Edi, whom you still love dearly (*charity*).

The balance of control

An additional problem for people with eating disorders is that their true sense of identity and self-worth is very low. They are fragile and appear childlike. On the other hand, their eating disorder bully is very strong. It is therefore a tightrope to balance between stepping back to let the non-eating disorder identity appear, and being bullied by the eating disorder. If you communicate in an overly dominant, assertive way, the tiny shoots of self-competence get stunted and the bully takes a tighter hold. In order to nurture this emerging sense of self, you need to step back into the non-expert submissive position when you are in conversation with Edi's true self – and yet hold a calm, firm, assertive approach when you are being shouted at or manipulated by the eating disorder bully.

This is a very difficult job and you may easily fall off the tightrope (professionals find this very difficult too). However, warmth always needs to be there, so that bit is easy. Use the wisdom of hindsight to reflect on these experiments.

Individual problems and solutions

 REFLECTION POINTS

1. Think now about appropriate limits and boundaries within your own situation: what appropriate limits and boundaries are needed to safeguard Edi? How will you set about doing it? If you have a husband or partner, you need to agree fully. You need to think about what sort of help you need from each other to stick to these rules over time. Take time to discuss fully your feelings, perceptions and difficulties arising from eating disorder behaviours, and if at all possible agree a joint way forward.

Single carers

Talking to people with similar experiences – a self-help group or telephone helpline – or a supportive GP, practice nurse or close friend, may be particularly helpful for single carers, who often have to cope alone.

2. Every family has different rules: what are the rules within your household? Think of as many aspects of family life as possible, the day-to-day accepted rules, and how they have been affected by the illness. For example, who does the cooking, the washing up, and who demands priority over the bathroom? Try to develop rules that are within your power to enforce. Can you explain to Edi and others (friends and family members who visit) *why* you think each rule is necessary? It does not have to be a logically argued case but it must have reason behind it.

ACTION POINT

Set aside time for yourself, and other involved close family members, to have a meeting with Edi when you can talk about your feelings and needs, as well as giving Edi time to describe what help and support she or he needs and wants from family members. Schedule the meeting so that everyone has time to prepare, to think about what problems they might want to raise.

The following ideas/rules may be useful at just such a meeting:

- Invite a family friend to act as a 'referee' to prevent emotional storms from derailing the discussion.

- Ensure that everyone has a turn to speak. Maybe this could be a role of the referee or an appointed 'chairperson'?

- Agree on a length of time that any one person may speak for. Perhaps ten minutes maximum in any one contribution to a discussion? Perhaps appoint one of the youngest family members as time-keeper, who indicates when ten minutes 'max individual talking time' are up?

- When interruptions are made, calmly remind those present that *everyone* will have a turn to speak.

- Encourage those present to adopt a step-by-step approach:

    Step 1 Explain your emotion/belief and attitude.

    Step 2 Explain what you need from the other person.

For example, a parent was feeling sick with worry and anxiety about her daughter's health, which had fallen into the amber region on the medical risk form (see Chapter 3). *'I am terrified about your physical health. I need to know that you are getting weighed by the practice nurse on a weekly basis and you are having your medical risk evaluated regularly.'*

Disagreements

Instead of a group 'disagreement', think more of an 'assertive discussion'. All family or group communication will include a certain amount of debate and conflict about all sorts of things. However, in supporting Edi it is even more important to try to avoid conversations becoming derailed by hostility and misunderstandings. Building an atmosphere of warmth and safety, free from destructive or hostile criticism, is essential, while at the same time not bending over backwards to keep the peace. Falling into the trap of accepting and being ruled by eating disorder behaviours can impede recovery. Take note of the following:

- Even a heated exchange is not always a disaster. Try to keep calm, repeat what you feel is important and then leave the topic.

- If an exchange becomes destructive/hurtful, acknowledge this and try to end it as soon as possible. When calm, return to the issue.

- If after some thought you feel your reaction has been less than helpful, be prepared to accept partial responsibility. For example: *'On reflection, I am sorry ...'* By being able to acknowledge and admit our own mistakes, we give others the important message that everyone is wrong at times as well as showing it is OK to be wrong sometimes. Again, every mistake is a treasure...

- Time out – if, despite your best efforts, emotions run high, it may be necessary to adjourn the meeting and start again when everyone is calm again. This could be after a 15-minute break, or the next day. Mutually agree on a time.

Medical rules

'Medical rules' as well as house rules are equally important in the context of eating disorders. In Chapter 3, we looked at medical risk. The discussion may be a pre-emptive measure, or be currently applicable to Edi's health. If the former, then open, honest discussion may serve as a motivational factor for Edi to try to avoid him- or herself deteriorating into a medically at-risk condition.

- It is recommended not to leave home and start university if either there is a high current medical risk or the risk of relapse is high.

- Driving is not recommended if there is high medical risk.*

Adopting new rules

Edi may rail against new rules, accusing you of trying to control him or her and using emotional blackmail. In such a situation, it is helpful to *sidestep any argument by calmly, firmly and clearly stating the reasons* for your thoughts and feelings – you may have to repeat this several times. Remind Edi of what was planned and discussed and *calmly repeat what you want*.

You may need to coach Edi about how to take up the new behaviours, using affirmation and positive framing as much as possible, e.g.:

> '*I know you are a person who does not want to neglect other people's needs. I need you to…*'

Communication skill 7: Reframing unhelpful thoughts

In order to be an effective carer, having a philosophical and reflective attitude about your own thoughts and assumptions is essential. Particularly as your thoughts – namely, anger and frustration towards the eating disorder – can often trigger unhelpful feelings and reactions towards Edi or other family members.

These misperceptions may be positively reframed by using optimism and compassion; contributing to an atmosphere of

---

* It is recommended that you suggest Edi lets the DVLA and their insurance agency know.

warmth and healing rather than despair and destruction. Not only is displaying anger and frustration towards the eating disorder damaging to your relationship with Edi, it will also deplete your energy reserves. In turn, Edi will feel guilty – at fault and responsible for all uncomfortable communication between the two of you. The cycle will keep turning *unless you can break it*.

Reframing thoughts is not easy. It is helpful to try to review your own progress in doing this, if possible in discussion with a supportive friend or professional. By thinking about them, discussing them, identifying possible problem areas in your own situation and being alert to these traps, you may be able to avoid them!

Examples are shown in Table 8.1 of how your thoughts, worries and comments may be reframed so that you can be as effective as possible in helping Edi.

TABLE 8.1 Reframing unhelpful thoughts

Unfavourable remarks about Edi's behaviour or personality 'Critical Comments'	More helpful comments
	Try to think of the 'crap sandwich' idea when responding to difficult behaviour. Remember the happier days before Edi took over, with Edi's current behaviour in the middle, and express your hope that with good support the happier days and behaviour will return. What more can you add to these responses?
'She hasn't got friends because she has alienated everyone.'	'She has lost all her friends because they could not cope with her illness.'
'She swears – her language is appalling. She even swears at me.'	'Using strong language must help her in some way. Perhaps it's her way of saying "I'm angry with life!"'
'He doesn't tell the truth any more.'	'This illness has made him unable to be honest.'

(continued)

TABLE 8.1 *continued*

'He fights me over everything – he is so selfish.'	*'The illness dominates all his thinking, and has taken over his life.'*

HOSTILITY

'I think that there is something wrong with her. She used to be pleasant but now she is anxious, nasty and vicious.'	*'She is so anxious, fearful and irritable. The eating disorder has meant that the pleasant part of her character is crowded out.'*
'She does it to hurt me.'	*'This illness is hurting me so much.'*
'She enjoys being difficult, she has destroyed the family.'	*'This illness has made her more difficult and it has really affected the whole family.'*
'He must see how much we are upset. He must hate us.'	*'I am upset by the illness. However, this illness is about his emotions and not mine and I must be as calm and warm as possible.'*

EMOTIONAL OVER-INVOLVEMENT

'I must invest the whole of my life into caring for Edi and making her life better. I must be there for her 24 hours every day.'	*'I need to ensure that the atmosphere at home is as warm and calm as possible. I need some time to nourish myself and the rest of the family, otherwise we will get drained and resentful.'*
'Food makes her so frightened. I cannot possibly let my husband be firm with her and insist that she eat even a small amount.'	*'There are some rules of living that have to be met. We have to eat to live. If she cannot look after her own nutritional needs, we have to take over this role.'*
'I must try and make her life as easy as possible by doing as much as I can for her. She is so fragile and emotional. If something goes wrong or is unexpected, she can't cope. It's best I'm there all the time.'	*'We have to help her be flexible and adaptable. She needs to master coping with slightly different approaches and rules.'*
'He is so uptight about cleanliness – I must let him have sole use of the kitchen so that he can finish his rituals.'	*'It is important that I do not collude with Edi in his obsessions as that keeps them going. The kitchen is a common area and must be kept as such.'*

DRAMATISATION OF EVENTS

'Seeing her and what she has been through – I have such an ache – I just want to cry all the time.'	*'It hurts to see all she has been through. I know I must remain strong for her, and calm to help her heal.'*

Communication skill 8: Discussing change and progress

People with eating disorders are rarely in what may be called 'Action' (see Chapter 7, 'Understanding change'). This means that large amounts of patience, effort and energy are needed to move an individual on from the 'Precontemplation' and 'Contemplation' positions, and acknowledge the problem behaviours, then prepare to turn their willpower towards positive change. It is therefore helpful to accept their mixed feelings – the ambivalence which is part of eating-disordered behaviour – rather than trying to argue logically in an effort to persuade, or to have a head-to-head confrontation (remember Rhino!).

Here are some sentence beginnings to help get you started in discussing change and progress. Try to be as positive as possible and focus on the work involved rather than the outcome:

> 'Sue, I can see how hard you're trying, you must be pleased that you managed to...'
>
> 'Peter, it can't have been easy to take that step...'
>
> 'Jane, it looks as if we may have been too optimistic with x goal, but if we remember every mistake is a treasure, what can we learn?...'

ACTION POINT

Think of particular behaviours causing difficulties in your own individual situation, and develop your own Useful Sentences.

Try to stress that the sufferer always has a CHOICE in their own life and that you will respect that choice (although you would not make the same choice in your own life, and may not completely understand someone else's choice).

Giving limited choices:

> *'It's up to you. If you're going to the cinema then you either have to have your snack before you go or after you get back, at dinner time with the family. Alternatively, you don't go to the cinema but have your snack at the usual time. You have to decide – it's about making a choice and compromising.'*
>
> *You could do this, or that, or maybe another thing –* in other words, you could eat before or after an activity, or at the usual time, but – as all human beings need to eat – there is no choice.

Small words can often be important. A key word to use often is AND rather than BUT when validating the mixed feelings Edi has about his or her eating disorder. BUT may be heard as rather judgemental. For example:

> *'Part of you says … (Edi talk) **and** yet part of you wants…' (a bigger non-eating disorder life)*
>
> *'On the one hand you think … (Edi talk) **and** on the other hand you…'*
>
> *'When you focus on you and the eating disorder in this moment, you feel … **and** when you reflect on the bigger picture…'*
>
> *'Zooming in on now, you … **and** if you take the broad life perspective you…'*

The use of **now, yet, at this moment** keeps the idea of change in the forefront as a realistic possibility. These small words can help bring people back from extremes:

> 'You do not think you are ready to ... **yet**'
>
> '**At the moment** you feel it's too difficult...'

Try to be respectful and to offer help in an open way, i.e. do not step in to give advice or generate all the solutions:

> 'I'd like to spend some time discussing/reflecting with you about ... When would be a good time for you? Is just now a good time?'
>
> 'I'd like to help. Tell me what I can do to help.'

Try to maintain an optimistic tone:

> 'Tomorrow is a new day – didn't beat it this time, try again tomorrow!'
>
> 'I have every confidence in you that tomorrow you can make things happen differently.'
>
> 'I was pleased that you tried. That means that we have gained knowledge.'

Try to find and practise your own Useful Sentences to help you grab any and every opportunity to support, encourage and motivate.

We hope that you will be able to avoid the following traps and pitfalls:

1. Dismissing or criticising other family members' experiences and actions.

2. Failing to take the feelings and concerns of other family members seriously.

3. Insisting on the correctness of your view of the problem which another family member does not accept (better to agree to differ).

4. Not listening and giving your attention.

5. Not providing support to other family members because your energy is so taken up with trying to help and support Edi.

6. Falling into reassurance traps with eating disorder behaviours.

7. Not recognising areas of competence, forgetting to give praise where due.

8. Giving advice before first getting permission to do so.

9. Not accepting that it will be in Edi's hands whether she or he works at getting better or not.

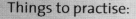

ACTION POINTS ➤

Things to practise:

- Maximising emotional intelligence.

- Remaining calm, consistent and compassionate.

- Listening well.

- Being clear, kind and gently persistent about what you want.

Reference list

1. Miller, W. and Rollnick, S. *Motivational Interviewing: Preparing people to change addictive behaviour.* New York: Guilford, 1991.
2. Miller, W. and Rollnick, S. *Motivational Interviewing.* New York: The Guilford Press, 2002.
3. Rollnick, S., Mason, P. and Butler, C. *Health Behaviour Change.* Edinburgh: Churchill Livingstone, 1999.

9

Caregiving relationships

This chapter focuses on the effects an eating disorder has on daily life and relationships, and how some of these patterns can keep the illness going.

Miscommunication in eating disorders

Individuals with eating disorders often suffer in silence. Hidden feelings, overwhelming emotions and powerful thoughts are often suppressed behind an expressionless mask (this may be a secondary effect from starvation or malnutrition). Others hide their pain behind a 'pleasing mask', taking care to put on a show as if everything is OK. Carers can instinctively respond to signals of bodily pain but, when trying to support a loved one with an eating disorder, are confused with the mismatch between face and body.

Stage 1: Interpersonal risk factors

Social factors play a key role. Interpersonal risk factors for eating disorders are shown in Figure 9.2a. People with eating disorders often display a heightened sensitivity to social judgement, a conscientious disposition and a tendency to strive for their personal best. When the illness develops, these traits become exaggerated and the 'personal best' becomes unrealistic – trying always to

FIGURE 9.1 Some put on a pleasing mask for the world. They may engage in a 'jolly conversational dance' which feels to others forced and unreal. This covers up the pain inside.

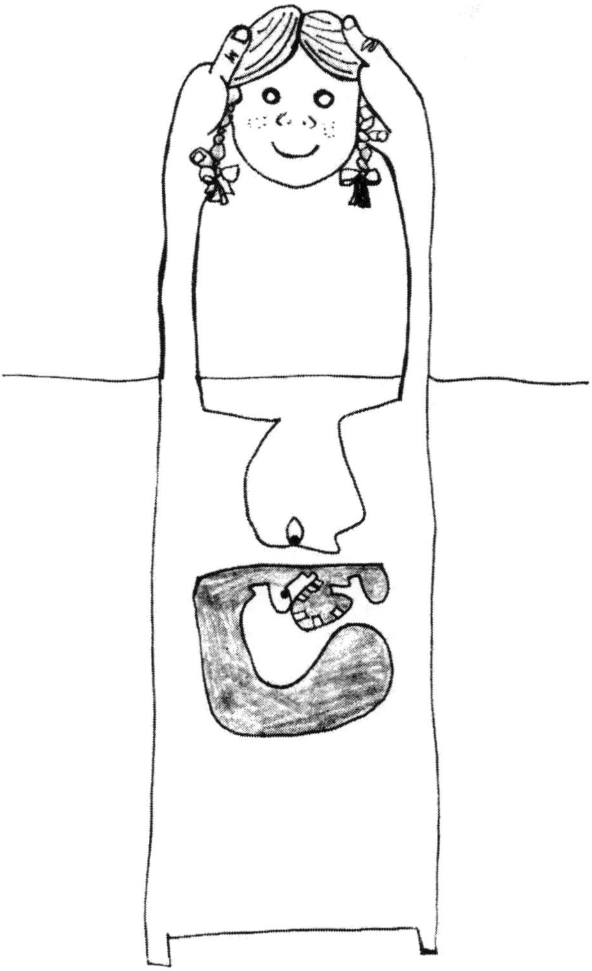

achieve 100 per cent, first place, a gold medal, size 0, with everything else seen as failure.

Edi's increased focus on striving for achievements in sport, dance or school may be seen as a positive for which they are praised. In Edi's eyes, the eating disorder helps to achieve these successes, whether academic, sporting or musical, which in turn contributes to the strongly held pro-illness belief: *My eating disorder makes me valued.*

These individual risk factors occur against a backdrop of current cultural obsessions with factors that lead to obesity (e.g. food and exercise), the idealisation of thinness, body shaming, fad diets and weight-based stigmatisation. These environmental factors have increased 'fat talk': unhealthy conversations about food, weight, body image and exercise that have become part of normal social interactions and peer bonding.

Society's focus on food and weight may have affected Edi personally – for example, Edi may have faced criticism, teasing and bullying about eating, weight and shape. As the illness develops, some of the symptoms of Edi's eating disorder may be seen by family, friends and society as positive – a slim figure, for example, which will be complimented. The sense of mastery over appetite can be rewarding. It signals an ability to do what most of the population today strives to do but often fail at abysmally: diet.

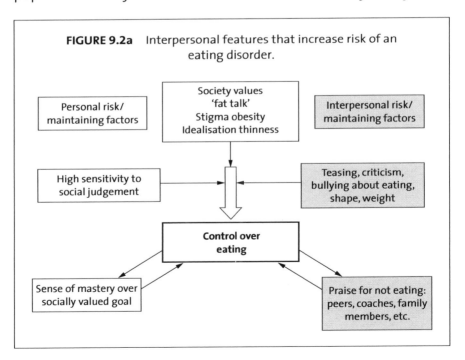

FIGURE 9.2a Interpersonal features that increase risk of an eating disorder.

caregiving relationships

However, this control over eating is unsustainable for life – the body and parts of the brain fight back and so this source of self-esteem is fragile. It comes with a heavy cost: despair and depression are always in the background.

Stage 2: Interpersonal maintaining factors

In Stage 2, there is a change in the behaviour of close others. Reactions to Edi change. These can be either emotional or taking action to try to stop Edi's disordered eating habits. Both these types of responses exaggerate Edi's symptoms, tightening the eating disorder's hold. Interpersonal maintaining factors for eating disorders are shown in Figure 9.2b.

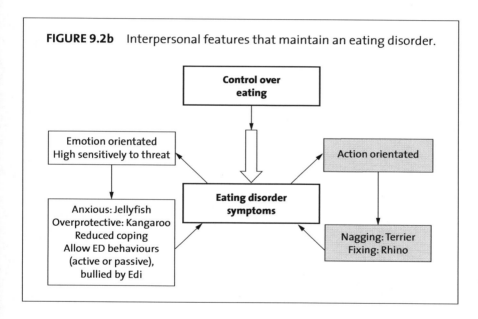

FIGURE 9.2b   Interpersonal features that maintain an eating disorder.

Edi's overt physical signs of starvation, changes in eating patterns and other associated behaviours can lead others to show concern and care. For instance, in anorexia nervosa, emaciation and physical frailty send a clear and powerful signal to others that something is seriously wrong. Again, emotional responses to bingeing and purging also send a powerful signal that something is very wrong. As Edi appears more vulnerable, people become drawn in to try to help. Here, the pro-eating disorder belief '*My eating disorder communicates distress*' comes to the forefront.

A natural reaction when someone is ill is to cosset them and make allowances for their behaviour. If the illness is short lived, this is normal and helpful, but in the case of eating disorders where the illness is protracted, it can lead to what is known as *accommodating* to the symptoms, further perpetuating the illness. This can reward Edi – who likes the special attention and continues with the behaviour. Carers who feel anxiety themselves are more prone to show these behaviours and become protective, like the Kangaroo.

Sometimes Edi's inner pain and emotional turmoil are less obvious. For example, Edi's face may not signal their inner state, leading them to appear aloof, as if they do not care. Alternatively, the behaviours of bulimia nervosa are often used to manage intense emotions, which are not obvious to other people. Cravings and compulsive behaviours (for example, eating the shopping intended for the whole family, possibly taking money to fund binges, shoplifting, creating mess in kitchen and bathroom) are all the external signs of Edi's inner pain. When the emotional pain is hidden, it is understandable for carers to feel exasperated by these behaviours and to be drawn into taking control. However, when done in the wrong way, Edi then feels threatened and resists change. This further frustrates others who may become critical and hostile, adding to the sense of threat and escalating into a vicious circle.

Whatever the eating disorder, or individual mix of eating disorders, carer responses are similar – a mix of helpful and unhelpful reactions. This is described in Chapter 5 on caring styles – Ostrich will try hard to keep the peace by avoiding acknowledgement of the problems, Rhino will rush in and try logical arguments, Kangaroo will try to protect. You may have already identified some of these behaviours in yourself. This chapter now builds on these metaphors, offering skills to overcome these instinctive reactions.

Interpersonal factors can maintain the illness

Trying to help someone with a severe eating disorder can feel rather like trying to walk a tightrope. High levels of stress in carers are common (Chapter 6, 'Stress, strain and developing resilience') and coping with that stress for long periods often leads to carers developing their own emotional problems. It is easy to fall into a reaction in which you display either too much or too little emotional response, be overly directive, underplay the eating disorders' effects on carers and family or try to 'do it all' for Edi. Finding the right, balanced approach is difficult and it is easy to fall into the snake pit of keeping the eating disorder going.

Getting the emotional balance right

Too much emotion – the Jellyfish

The Jellyfish metaphor is useful to describe being in a raw emotional state with all feelings close to the surface. A Jellyfish may be swept away by currents of emotion and beliefs (which may or may not be accurate). You may dissolve into tears, become frozen with fear, agitated with doubt, erupt into rage or, in an anxious state, constantly check up on Edi. (Edi also may be beset with intense emotional responses.) These intense, visible reactions have an impact on everyone in your environment. Heightened family reactions to eating-disordered behaviour may contribute to Edi's feelings of rejection, feeling ashamed and to blame. Despite knowing that the behaviour is causing distress, Edi feels unable to change it. Sufferers may withdraw completely from family life. Despite positive intentions stemming from concern, a high emotional response from carers may lead to an *increase* in eating disorder behaviours.

As discussed in Chapter 8, 'Communication', it is very important to work to modify your own emotional reactions. The skills in Chapter 11 will help you to make a start, but you may need additional, sometimes professional, input in order to help Edi effectively.

Too little emotion – the Ostrich

Some carers swing to the other extreme, attempting to disengage and cut off from the problems caused by the eating disorder. They feel heartbroken to see Edi so ill, in great distress and possibly in poor physical health. They know that talking about food and other pertinent issues causes outbursts and tension. To avoid confrontations and to distract themselves from personal distress, they may stay away as much as possible – for example, at work, in hobbies or activities outside the home, socialising with friends, perhaps at a pub or club. It is of course extremely important for carers to take time to recharge and relax, but these activities should not be used in place of facing the illness.

By trying to ignore the problems, the Ostrich, with its head in the sand, runs the risk of colluding with the eating disorder. (Edi also uses lots of avoidance, Ostrich-type behaviours.) Ultimately, avoidance negatively impacts on many aspects of family life: while others are left to shoulder even more of the care burden, the Ostrich may experience high levels of guilt. At the same time, eating disorder symptoms worsen, and the family becomes even more lonely and isolated.

It may be that you simply don't know where to start in trying to help Edi. Again, using APT can help and the 'first steps' outlined in Chapter 4 are a starting point.

The 'just so' balance of emotional reaction – the St Bernard approach

When your emotions are welling up or fizzing, consider trying some of the following strategies:

- Take a step back, put the emotion somewhere else (imagine it in your toe and watch it) or take yourself somewhere else (on the ceiling or in a safe calm place so you can 'watch yourself from above or on a screen').

- Breathe in, count to 10 and let it out on a count to 12.

- Switch into 'emotional intelligence' mode. Listen and tune into Edi's behaviour, understanding that it is a cry for help.

- Summon up the image of a St Bernard dog. Do not engage the eating disorder in a shouting match – you may cause an avalanche. Do not get paralysed by despair and turn away, avoiding the problem. Instead, set out to reach Edi before they get further lost in the frozen wastes of the eating disorder. You can provide warmth and nurturance, and can stay with them until change occurs.

The St Bernard is reliable, steady and dependable by nature, even when a situation is treacherous. The St Bernard's loyalty and compassion are infinite – even after battling in gale-force conditions, he can offer love and protection. He is warm, soft and comforting. He remains calm, collected and follows the job he has been trained to do. Similar to caring for Edi, extra input is often needed.

Getting the directional balance right

Too little direction – the 'Kangaroo care' response … trying to do it all for Edi

When someone is obviously so ill, unhappy and distressed, it is very easy to be drawn into trying to protect completely, to create a 'pouch' of care to keep ordinary problems and experiences at bay for the sufferer. (Edi may also be highly sensitive to threat – as Kangaroos often are.) Also, Kangaroos often share high standards with Edi – in this case they have high standards and expectations about their parenting role. Rather than *guiding* Edi about choices and possible courses of action, this overprotective response takes away opportunities for personal development and for exploring the world. It has a reciprocal effect on the person with the eating disorder who becomes an 'Ostrich', avoiding his or her responsibilities. This type of reaction is common for people who have prolonged periods of face-to-face contact with Edi, including nurses on inpatient units.

At home, some carers try to become 'super-carers' and martyr themselves to the eating disorder and can sacrifice themselves (and sometimes the family) to help the sufferer – willing to drive for miles to find the 'right' brand of cereal, available to talk for hours at any time regardless of other matters needing attention, organising work for Edi, paying off bills, spending hours looking for the 'perfect flat' and possibly flatmates too for the sufferer and so on. Rather than helping, this type of accommodating and enabling behaviour often has the opposite effect. Consciously or unconsciously, Edi may come to the conclusion that it is their illness that 'rewards' them with this attention and special treatment. They believe that without the illness they would not be protected, doted on, given time – and in view of these perceived positive benefits are reluctant to give up the illness. By adhering to Edi's rigid needs, a carer further reinforces the dependency and lack of responsibility. This is followed by even greater demands from Edi for special care, leading again to even greater efforts by the carers.

Accommodating Edi's behaviour may leave him or her in total control. They may dictate and influence any number of the following:

- the type of crockery used at meals

- how crockery is cleaned

- what time food is eaten

- where food is eaten

- exactly what is eaten

- what foods are kept in the house

- how the kitchen is cleaned

- how food is stored

- how food is prepared – cooking and ingredients

- how much and what exercise they take

- how their body shape or weight is monitored

- how the house is cleaned and tidied

- what other family members do and for how long in the kitchen and bathroom

- what other family members do in other rooms in the house, and at what times

- what other family members can talk about in front of her or him.

In an effort to be a peacemaker, carers may choose to ignore the aspects of Edi's behaviour that impinge on family life. For example, if Edi suffers with bulimia, nothing may be said in spite of food disappearing, money being taken or kitchen and bathroom areas being left in a mess. Carers may get caught in prolonged ruminations and endless discussions centred on 'eating disorder talk'. They give reassurance in an attempt to relieve Edi's panic-stricken state about whether:

- she or he will get fat

- it is safe or acceptable to eat a certain food

- she or he looks fat in certain clothes

- she or he is ugly/unlovable/selfish/boring/useless/ unintelligent, etc.

These super-efforts added to exhaustion associated with caring for Edi may lead eventually to burnout for the carer, or understandable outbursts of frustration and anger, especially when other family members protest about neglect of their needs. Edi is left feeling unsure of reactions which seem to swing between super-care and protection to inexplicable (to Edi) sudden withdrawal. In an attempt to avoid their own negative feelings and seemingly out of control emotional responses of others, Edi then retreats further into their eating disorder, rigidly sticking to their own individual eating disorder 'rules'.

Breaking out of Kangaroo care

It is not easy to break out of the vicious cycle of accommodating and enabling the illness. However, as we discussed in the Preface, changing your own behaviour is an important first step. You may need to reduce your own expectations of what you offer – in other words, step back and close the pouch a bit! Change is more likely to occur if people feel they are free to make their own choices. Overcoming obstacles and problems for oneself, no matter how small, is the most successful booster for confidence. Remaining enclosed in the pouch means Edi never has the opportunity to make choices, regain lost confidence and rebuild self-esteem.

Too directive a response: Rhinoceros response

'Rhinoceros Response' involves trying to present logical arguments to Edi as to why she or he should change, either through coercion or by presenting ways in which Edi should change. This may arise if you have a rather detailed analytical approach to problem solving (these traits can be genetic and may match those of Edi). However, when presented with constant arguments for change and directions on how to change, Edi is given opportunities to rehearse and articulate arguments for *not* changing, further driving Edi's disordered eating behaviour. The eating disorder, *which does not respond to logic*, persists. While the carer will be left feeling defeated, frustrated, drained and angry, Edi will leave these battles with renewed power and energy. At the same time, Edi may be left feeling rejected, unloved, not understood or contemptuous because someone close to them, whom they trust, has dictated forcefully how exactly and why they should change. Neither the Rhino carer nor the eating disorder is willing to back down, leading to a spiral of coercion, frustration and anger. Other family members may be drawn in, responding with sarcasm, teasing or mocking the rituals, leading to further deterioration in home relationships.

The psychological rule of resistance is: *If you order and direct people to change when they are not ready to do so, it can have the opposite effect: they dig their heels in – a counter-motivational effect.* This is especially true in eating disorders where beliefs, no matter how distorted they seem to anyone else, are rigidly held with strong and abnormal emotional meaning (this is visibly illustrated by brain scan results).

Surprisingly, extreme examples of coercive behaviour amongst professionals have been seen on ED inpatient wards. Where isolation, deprivation, lack of privileges and nasogastric feeding have all failed to persuade the sufferer to give up their illness, the staff have resorted to encasing arms in plaster. Innocently, all these measures are done in an effort to save life, to care and in the sufferer's 'best interest'. Unfortunately, such measures also serve to create extreme resentment in the sufferer, who still will not change her or his behaviour on release.

Remember, it is a natural human reaction to rebel if you think that your freedom is being curtailed. Thus a common response if someone tries to force you to change your mind is to become more firmly determined not to. Edi feels that she or he is not being listened to and becomes more aroused and irritable, and digs their heels in even deeper. Instead, it is important for you to calmly agree to disagree and assertively implement clear limits and boundaries.

Escaping 'Rhino responsibility'

Try to step back and agree to differ.

> *'I don't see things the way you do, I can't agree with you. But I accept that's how you feel.'*

Walk away from arguments calmly.

> *'I can see you are upset/angry just now – let's discuss this later when we are both calm.'*

Let it be, do not join in ... Not easy – this applies to trying to change all personal coping styles!

Finding the right balance

The most effective treatments for eating disorders have been found to involve all family members working together to help their loved one. Getting alongside to encourage and support Edi's efforts, and offering praise wherever possible for all efforts and achievements, can do wonders in recovery.

The 'just so' Balance of mentoring – the 'determined Dolphin' approach

Dolphins have been recorded swimming alongside boats to guide them through difficult straits and helping swimmers in the water get to safety. Following on from our descriptions of Kangaroo Care, Rhino Response and Ostrich Approach (carers may think of other recognisable patterns of behaviour), perhaps families could discuss a Determined Dolphin helping Edi towards the safety of recovery.

This means having a good balance of warmth and guidance, sometimes getting ahead of Edi to lead through a safe passage. Dolphin is there as a guide alongside Edi, trusting their ability to swim out of the situation, sometimes remaining behind to allow Edi to take the lead or, when needed, moving ahead and being a little more directive, outlining good life choices. Mostly, Dolphin will be gently nudging, staying close and watching closely, remaining alongside until the person reaches the safety of recovery. Then, Dolphin will leave the person to continue on their way, the main aim being that person's well-being.

As in facing any difficult challenge, setbacks will be inevitable in the struggle against the illness, and carers can play an essential part in encouragement to keep on trying – with recognition and praise for all efforts:

> *'Well done! I can see you tried really hard.'*

REFLECTION POINTS

1. Beware of falling into an extreme emotional reaction – 'Jellyfish' or 'Ostrich'. Carers need to remain calm, warm, nurturing and consistent, like a St Bernard.

2. Beware of getting too frightened and drawn into accommodating eating disorder behaviour, being controlled and bullied by it – Kangaroo. It is impossible to hold this position *consistently* – at times Kangaroo will react with an emotional backlash (in other words, lose your calm).

3. Using logical, analytical, detailed argument or irony, sarcasm or mockery – Rhinoceros – is also unhelpful. No matter how good the intentions and motivation, trying to force someone into change will lead to strong resistance. If you argue over the details, you will lose sight of the big picture.

4. Aim to keep the pattern of interactions as *consistent* as possible over time and between all family members, while guiding like a Dolphin.

5. Beware of times when you and/or Edi are tired, hungry or emotionally depleted as you will not have the energy to take a mature perspective. At these times, step back if you can.

6. *Mistakes can be treasures.* Learn from mistakes or setbacks. If you have an unfortunate interaction, apologise, move on and get back on track *'I am sorry, I ... I was tired ... I should have said/done...'*

10

Social relationships: partners, siblings and peers

We have explained how the brain is altered by starvation, making it very hard for people with eating disorders to change by themselves (Chapter 2). This section gives more detail about this and considers its impact on different types of relationships (e.g. partners, siblings, young carers).

Innate social rewards

Touch and taste are two innate rewards in animals, both of which are disrupted in people with eating disorders. In infancy, touch – the comfort and safety we experience in the presence of others – is a preferred reward and takes precedence over food. For example, in an experiment using monkeys, the experimental psychologist Harlow found that infant monkeys preferred soft, furry, maternal models over a wire model where there was food. Touch is thought to be one of the main ways that individual well-being and group cohesion are formed. In humans, humour, laughter, playing and talking together are important parts of the social glue that promotes well-being. This soothing system appears to be less strong in people with eating disorders.

The social brain in eating disorders

In starvation, social functioning is disrupted and may account for the following features that have been found in people with eating disorders:

- less accuracy and sensitivity in reading the emotions of others
- reduced expression of emotion – a flat poker face[1]
- sensitisation to signals of threat
- desensitisation to signals of kindness and compassion
- sensitisation to signals of perceived power and dominance of others, with a tendency to judge oneself negatively
- a lack of trust in others and difficulties feeling safe and secure in relationships.

All of these make social interactions difficult. A root cause of this might be lower levels of the hormone oxytocin, an organiser of social behaviour. Also, the chemistry of reward (dopamine, serotonin, oxytocin, cannabinoid and opiate brain systems) may be out of balance. This disrupts social reward, leading to social isolation. Loneliness activates the threat system, which makes people even more wary and suspicious. A vicious circle develops so that sufferers become more locked into the eating disorder. Strengthening relationships is an important stepping stone to recovery.

Advanced social complexity: Peer and partner relationships

The social part of the brain is highly sophisticated and requires a large amount of brainpower.[2] This is because it takes a great deal of sophistication to synchronise your behaviours with those of another person and understand others' thoughts, drives, desires and perspectives. Several different terms are used to describe this in psychology, including theory of mind, mentalising and social cognition. This skill gradually develops during childhood and becomes more complex – for example, you are thinking about someone thinking about you, who in turn is thinking about how you are thinking about them ... and so on.

The skills involved in 'theory of mind' include:

- reading the emotional state of another person from verbal and non-verbal cues

- using non-verbal signs and communication style to show someone that you are listening

- being able to empathise with someone else's emotional state, and understand what the other person needs as a result of that emotional state – in other words, being able to put yourself in their shoes; this may involve help with emotional regulation (both expressing and containing emotions) or more practical problem solving

- being able to alter your behaviour to take into account the reaction of the other person.

Of course the skills of 'theory of mind' are, in essence, mind-reading, which can go wrong if underlying attitudes, assumptions and prejudices differ. A clear example is if someone says to Edi, 'You look well'. Because of the voice of 'fat talk' in Edi's mind, they interpret this as the other person saying they are fat. Rather than being pleased by the comment, Edi feels upset. Mind-reading is difficult if non-verbal emotional signals are inhibited (such as when there is a flat, expressionless face as in eating disorders).

Relationships can be ruptured if theory of mind is out of step. Once you become aware this has happened, use the APT approach to take steps to repair the relationship. Acknowledge that something has gone wrong and that mistakes have been made. The good news is that working to build upon misunderstandings can strengthen the relationship in the long run.

FIGURE 10.1 The poker face mask of anorexia nervosa. People with eating disorders have reduced emotional expression – a mask or poker face. This contrasts with an intense, overwhelming inner emotional state.

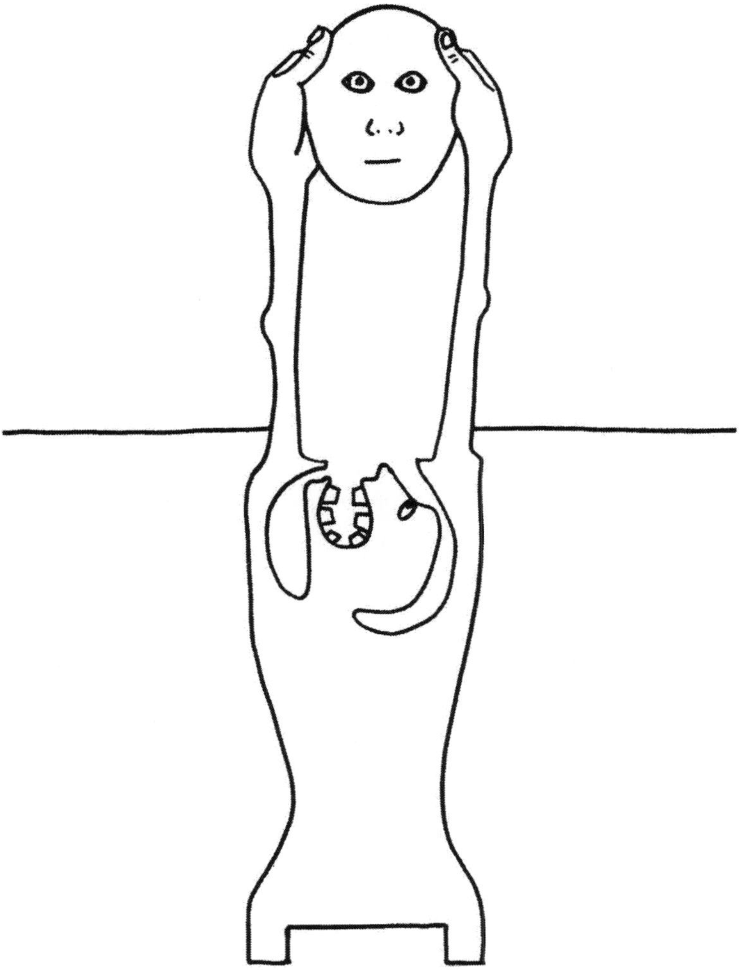

The partner relationship

Being a partner of someone with an eating disorder is somewhat different to being a parent, sibling or other relation. Ideally a healthy partner relationship should be one between two equal adults: both partners are entitled to have input, and choices that benefit the relationship are often prioritised. When an eating disorder is present, it is as if there are *three* people in the relationship. You may feel ostracised and isolated from Edi. Further, as you face these challenges, loyalty and respect about the relationship's privacy may make it more difficult for you to ask for help and support from others. Without this safety valve, partners experience high levels of stress.

You may feel anxious, depressed, hopeless, irritable and angry at the slightest provocation. You may cut yourself off from pleasant activities and become less active. At times you may adopt a more Rhino style with a forceful, authoritarian manner. Your own anxiety may lead you to avoid triggering situations which provoke Edi's anxiety. However, in order to recover from an eating disorder, Edi needs to recognise problems, face fears and master their anxiety. It is helpful if you have support to have the courage to do the same thing. Openly discussing your fears, frustrations and feelings with your partner not only paves the way for you to get help but it also models the need for connection and intimacy with other people. This is a helpful life strategy, but one which may have been lost by people with an eating disorder. Without using healthy emotion regulation strategies, difficult emotions can build up and develop into unhelpful patterns of interaction, such as becoming a Rhino or a Jellyfish.

Some typical comments about relationship problems with partners:

> *'At times I was at breaking point, I had never been under pressure like it, I didn't understand it. I couldn't understand how someone who claimed to love me could be so hostile to me.'*

> *'If we include putting up with snappy behaviour which I know is provoked by the fact that she feels full, I usually let it slide as opposed to pick her up on it, which is not what I usually do … tolerating a lot of bad moods that I had done nothing at all to bring about…'*

You may notice problems in some of the following areas (or some such transition).

Physical intimacy

The physical aspect of the relationship is usually severely interrupted because of both decreased libido and problems with body image. Well-meaning compliments intended to build confidence and self-esteem are put down. In a relationship without an eating disorder, complimenting on a partner's clothes or appearance is common place, but Edi will not be able to accept such admiration and will sometimes aggressively refute comments. Comments unrelated to size or shape, such as eye makeup or hair, are sometimes safer territory.

> *'I know she is feeling bad … You know, when curled up in bed I will keep my hand on her leg and nowhere near her stomach, this sort of thing. That's become a habit, I guess, a learnt response.'*
>
> *'It devastated me when any remark I made about her clothes would be met with more self-deprecating comments. When I explained how upset it made me that she thought of herself like that, she didn't vocalise her beliefs so much after that. I think this then helped her negative beliefs not to be reinforced in her mind.'*

Social life

Your social life may have become severely disrupted by the illness, isolating you as a couple.

> *'I am going to see a friend, who she likes very much, at a pizzeria and this place has big pizzas and she is not going. Even if she ordered something else it would be too stressful for her and she wouldn't enjoy it.'*
>
> *'We will try and perhaps go for drinks only.'*
>
> *'I always made excuses as to why she couldn't be there. My friends hadn't seen us as a couple for years. They must have thought something was wrong but nobody ever said anything'*
>
> *'We only go on holiday once a year and when we do it's a stressful experience and once or twice in the past we have come home a day or two early because it has just gotten too much.'*
>
> *'She is very determined to eat but we have ways of working round it now. She will look in the guide books. For example, when we are in Spain we nearly always have tapas, there are no great big piles of it, and we will eat when she wants to eat. As far as I am concerned this is a small concession to make.'*

Relationship breakdown

You may make a decision to finish the relationship – it is not helpful to use the threat of separation as an ultimatum to force change. However, in some cases, separation can be in the best interest of both parties but due consideration is needed to take into account the secondary difficulties and change in personality that result from the eating-disordered state.

'Parents have an unconditional love if they have a kid, whereas, you know, don't get me wrong, we are still together, and that in itself demonstrates an incredible bond between us. But you know love for girlfriends, boyfriends, is probably not unconditional and can be worn down by horrible behaviour.'

Supporting recovery

If you are the partner of someone with an eating disorder, you will need high levels of emotional intelligence as well as resilience and patience to keep the relationship in place. This means first acknowledging and dealing with your own feelings. Remember – Edi's brain will be in starvation and malnutrition mode, and may swing from appearing like a bland ice queen with no flicker of emotion on their face to extreme irritability and outbursts of temper in a very short space of time.

Some family members, as part of their effort to help and support, take on the role of an 'emotional Geiger counter' and become very aware of changes in Edi's feelings. Awareness of these signals can register what help and support might be needed. Go through the APT routine and plan how you will broach any difficult situation or subject. You may find it helpful to script it out beforehand. As we have outlined, sandwiching the problem between supportive signals can reduce arousal and aid listening.

'Our relationship is very important to me. I have noticed that you have become more irritable recently. I would like to explore this so that together we can explore what needs to be done to make you more comfortable. Is this a good time to talk about it? Or maybe you can suggest a better time?'

The needs of both partners have to be taken into consideration when moving towards recovery. This is important for the sake of the relationship and also for the development and growth of a sense of responsibility and independence once the eating disorder identity is left behind. It is easy for a very supportive partner to fall, inadvertently, into a parental, Kangaroo-type role. This distorts the relationship, which becomes unequal, with a dependent patient and an overprotective therapist/parent figure. This inhibits the maturation of the relationship and interrupts the natural course of development where responsibility flows from the individual, helping to build the relationship, and into wider roles of nurturing children, with friends and in the community. The motivational and communication style of nudging and providing more than one option to choose from allows you to work together as a relationship of equals.

There are a variety of ways in which suggestions can be made:

'How can I help you? I can do this or do that (two options are better than one) What do you think? Do you have other suggestions?'

'Let's look at the pros and cons together, because many times you know better than me. I can learn from you, and you can learn from me.'

'As a team we'll always work better than separately.'

'We can talk about it now, or later, when we eat, take a walk, after TV, before going to bed. How do you feel about that? Which would you prefer?'

Clear planning is critical. The default position is that the eating disorder habit will rule, so predicting obstacles, and visualising and vocalising practical solutions several times is helpful.

> '*Let's use our brains when they're fresh at the start of the day to talk through what the meal plan is for the day and how I can help. Can you think of any problems that might come up? Let's try to anticipate obstacles and think it through so that we have solutions to break through the eating disorder's dangerous habits.*'

A regular time for reflection and review is a critical part of this process.

> '*Let's set aside time to chat and reflect about how it has gone and think of any readjustments that might be needed. We can keep in touch by phone, or a text is ok, but we need to keep our eye on the bigger picture too, make sure your eating disorder doesn't reappear.*'

The trap of reassurance giving and accommodation

Caregivers often try to avoid or alleviate Edi's distress by allowing eating disorder behaviours to rule and dominate the relationship. The technical term for this is 'accommodating'. It can happen so automatically that you may not realise what you are doing. You may protect Edi from the negative consequences by moderating those consequences or trying to remove them. The technical term for this is 'enabling'. Also, some partners fall into the trap of providing a large amount of reassurance. It can be easier for partners to fall into this pattern of behaviour, easier even than for parents because of the expectations associated with the role. Also when you are a lone carer, it can be harder to step back and reflect about what is going on.

The following are the kinds of scenarios that can develop:

Accommodating Edi's anxiety:

> 'Cooking bacon does stress her … When I do, I make sure to open all the windows or doors and things. We don't cook bacon often.'

Continual reassurance-seeking:

> 'Have you rinsed the pasta or the rice?'

If you notice that this pattern has developed, go to your APT skills. In the first instance, it may be helpful to just keep track of what, when and how it occurs (AWARENESS). Are there times you feel manipulated/blackmailed/bullied, etc.?

Keeping a journal will allow you to calmly reflect on this pattern away from the heat of the moment. The distance and physical presence that a written account provides allows you both to develop a different perspective and have an overview. If you are stuck in cycles with these types of behaviours, the first step is to choose which goal it makes sense to prioritise. Next, the plan to change will need a lot of work. The steps involved need to be discussed, explained and PLANNED for.

You need to carefully choose your time to discuss it with your partner. This will be painful for you both so you need to set up the environment so that it provides as much comfort, calmness and reassurance as possible. You can refer them to the scientific information and discuss how accommodating or 'giving in to the eating disorder bully, or minx' is harmful in the long term. This should be done in a kind, matter of fact, but gentle tone, with the understanding that the 'eating disorder bully' has to be identified and recognised as separate from the individual. Some people find metaphors helpful, such as talking to the 'recovery part/mindset' rather than the 'eating disorder minx, part, voice, mindset, habit, bully'.

TRY the change and use this as a source of reflection and learning. You may get a backlash from Edi when you start to discuss these issues; be prepared for this.

Maybe you need to accept the possibility that you were doing things too quickly? It is difficult to judge the level of terror associated with change because of Edi's lack of social signalling. *Remember* – shouldering the blame, and showing that you are not afraid to accept and take the blame for your mistakes, can be a helpful way to take away the paralysing straight jacket of self-blame and criticism which encourages and stokes the eating disorder.

The sibling relationship

With eating disorders commonly appearing in teens and early twenties, there may be siblings in the family. Siblings differ from parents in the way that they experience the eating disorder. They are not in a position of responsibility, but the strong interpersonal consequences of the illness draw them in. Siblings can get excluded and overlooked because of the high level of anxiety in the active phase of the illness, with parents focused on doing everything they can to support Edi. A sibling relationship can extend over a shared lifetime and so strengthening rather than neglecting this bond is very important. Siblings offer a unique resource in that they knew Edi before the illness and are also a part of the same peer cohort. They can be in a good position to help repair the interpersonal disconnection that occurs when Edi appears.

Depending on the age of siblings, sometimes parents can offer appropriate information, skills and support to help them understand the eating disorder. In some cases, it may be helpful for siblings – perhaps along with Edi – to discuss with professionals their worries and concerns about how to offer support. Again dependent on age, siblings may be part of round-the-table family conferences when the problems caused for the family by the eating disorder (for instance, the problems of access to the only bathroom in the house) are discussed openly. Young people, when given the opportunity, can often come up with very practical suggestions.

The problems with social relationships which may precede and/or be accentuated by the illness can cause problems for Edi as well as for their friends. Edi may calibrate their behaviours against other people and/or compete or compare with siblings. In the active phase of the illness, this can take the form of eating less and exercising more.

Calibration and competition

People with eating disorders have an automatic tendency to compare themselves negatively to others. It is as if their sense of self-competence, self-acceptance and security – for example, the thought 'I am good enough' – is poorly developed. Instead, Edi may have developed an unhelpful and damaging tendency to rely upon the opinion, respect and love of others. This often manifests as scanning the environment for cues to confirm what they already believe: 'You are *not* good enough'. They are hypersensitive to criticism and insensitive to praise or acceptance. These tendencies become heightened when the eating disorder develops. It means that Edi monitors eating and exercise behaviours in others. All the biological forces that their body switches on to make them eat are transferred into preparing food for others or making others eat. They can get angry if others reject this or do not want to eat.

> *Julie and Jane described how their sister would come home from school and leave large amounts of snack foods around the kitchen tempting them to eat.*
>
> *Pauline was rather ambivalent about her older sister's habit of giving her money in order to buy snacks from the tuck shop at school. 'Well, if she wants to give me money – why not?'*

> *Susan was frustrated by the mealtime rows that emerged when she had a flu-like illness and did not want to eat as she had no appetite or sense of taste.*
>
> *Peggy was mortified by her sister's dress at school. 'It is as if she is flaunting her thinness – it's disgusting.'*

'Parental siblings'

Once an eating disorder develops, younger siblings may overtake Edi in terms of emotional intelligence and maturity. This may mean that they can step into the parental role. Whilst aspects of this can be helpful (e.g. monitoring snacks), it can have its downside as it breaks a healthy sibling relationship. It can also lead to the sibling trying to care for the rest of the family

> *'I essentially became the carer for the carers in my family. I saw my family going to pieces around me, and felt like it was my responsibility to fix it. I didn't have the responsibility my parents did to maintain my sister's health, but instead I felt I had the responsibility to maintain the family structure as a whole.'*

Guilt, fear and shame

Guilt and shame are common emotions felt both by Edi and by other family members. This can be a toxic brew.

> *'My own personal emotions were affected by the eating disorder. I felt guilty, not only from some of the anger directed towards me, but also as if I were somehow at fault for the family falling apart – or at least that I had failed at fixing it.'*

> '*Also there was the fear of becoming like my sister. For me, this manifested in a pressure to always be the opposite of her during that time – the happy, positive, healthy and strong one. But ironically, I think that because of genetic or environmental factors, I am actually predisposed to some of the same characteristics – so I have struggled between the identity/role placed on me by others (and by myself) and some of my own thoughts, feelings, and corresponding needs.*'

Neglect or the negative atmosphere for the unaffected siblings

The increased time and attention paid to Edi usually means that other siblings are somewhat neglected and exposed to highly negative atmosphere. In some cases, this can lead to other siblings developing their own emotional problems. Others leave home early.

> '*I didn't exactly feel jealous of the attention she was getting, but I did feel the effects of all the energy spent on her. My parents, exhausted and frustrated by caring for and fighting with her, were more on edge around me, and sometimes lashed out more than they would otherwise. In that sense, it wasn't so much that I was getting less attention from them, but that I was getting more negative attention.*'

The breakdown of the sibling relationship

All of the factors discussed contribute to the fragmentation of the sibling relationship. The following case history demonstrates one manifestation:

> '*The first way that I was affected by my sister's anorexia was the relationship between us. We were never really close, but when she retreated into her eating disorder world, our relationship became non-existent. In the full year after she was diagnosed, in addition to the months leading up to it,*

> *I honestly think we had only one conversational interaction. We didn't fight (though we had frequently fought before the illness), it was just complete silence and emotional separation. The avoidance was most likely two-way. On one hand, I was too young to understand what was really going on and was actually very afraid of it all. I wouldn't have known what to say even had I been brave enough to try.'*

Sometimes the personality makeup and the associated values of siblings can diverge so much that being bosom friends is impossible. Having too high an expectation about what to expect from siblings may cause problems. Family members may need to step back and see the bigger picture – there will be a lifetime for a relationship but it may be necessary to have your needs for intimacy and warmth met by others.

Siblings supporting recovery

Some siblings find it helpful to use the motivational interviewing communication style with reflective listening skills – the 'LESS-is-more' approach.

> *'I think talking about what's for dinner later is upsetting you. Would you like to finish off watching the film we started the other day instead?'*
>
> *'It must be really horrible for you to have all those thoughts about yourself.'*
>
> *'Shall we carry on making those Christmas cards together as I can hear that you're getting anxious? It would make us both feel better I think.'*
>
> *'I would really like to timetable some time to talk together about my travel plans – you are great at getting organised. Can we do it next Sunday evening?'*

Additionally, because of the different nature of a sibling–sibling relationship, the focus of interactions and conversation content can be helpfully focused on age-appropriate topics – music, television, films, difficulties with relationships, etc. This is an important role as siblings can be a bridge to help connections with the world outside the eating disorder and also signal that challenges and mistakes occur but can be faced and overcome.

REFLECTION POINTS

1. The eating disorder can provoke hostile competition and even 'bullying' with siblings. It is important to recognise that this is the illness and the damage it causes to brain function. This is not the 'real' Edi, but a starved lonely brain which is turned into primitive threat mode by the eating disorder. This pattern will abate with recovery.

2. Restoring and repairing sibling relationships will be a key goal. Sharing information and skills with siblings in an appropriate way for their age and stage of development can help this process.

3. It is important not to neglect the needs of siblings. *All* of the recovery team needs to care and be kind and compassionate to themselves and each other. Setting aside time for high-quality activities is of great importance.

4. Siblings can be a wonderful resource, especially in terms of combating isolation and disconnection from others.

5. Siblings hopefully will share a similar life span and so repairing any illness-related ruptures will be of key importance as a resource for life.

The friend relationship

Friends may be uncertain how to respond to Edi, who has lost the ability to join in, whose thinking is distorted and often illogical, who has lost their sense of humour and fun, and who does not want to participate in activities shared in the past. Friends may be unsure how to respond or feel afraid of saying the wrong thing, causing them to stay away. Additionally, social interactions often centre around food (e.g. going out for dinner or having a lunch date together), making Edi shy away from arranging or joining in social commitments. Edi becomes isolated, losing support structures and a sounding board to check out ideas, further perpetuating negative self-deprecating thoughts. The distorted eating disorder thinking thus dominates more and more. These patterns are often difficult to break.

Giving caring friends relevant information about the illness and about eating-disordered thinking and behaviour can help them understand more about Edi's behaviour and help repair relationships. Where long-term friendships have survived, those relationships are often strengthened by the shared feelings of tackling a very difficult project – beating the eating disorder.

Friends can be an invaluable resource in helping Edi gradually regain an understanding of non-eating disorder life and activities, starting with short periods of shared activity – for example, watching a short TV programme together, doing a jigsaw, playing cards/a board game, then gradually building up time together, and then helping Edi to re-establish other social connections.

Protecting the well-being of all carers

The first step in protecting the well-being of carers is to be aware and recognise the impact an eating disorder may have on the family. Keep an eye out for the following symptoms:

- Physical effects: tense aching muscles, headaches, sweating, cold clammy hands, palpitations, dry mouth, nausea, susceptibility to infections.

- Mental effects: difficulty concentrating, absent-mindedness, loss of humour.

- Emotional effects: depression, nervousness, anxiety, agitation, poor self-image, feelings of shame and failure.

- Unhealthy changes in behaviour: insomnia, anger outbursts, increased smoking or drinking, isolating.

Once you have become AWARE of stress reactions, the next step is to talk about it and to make PLANS to remediate these problems (remember APT). And of course, reflect on how these reactions affect others in the home and discuss what could help. For example, try to find regular times to have a break, possibly attend a regular class – art, creative writing, a choir, etc. – or join another social group while others take over for a while. Review the situation regularly.

Single carers – a parent, a partner, a sibling – who shoulder all responsibility at home when Edi becomes ill, especially when they live in a rural area, may come close to complete breaking point. Finding a way to have a break of any kind can seem an impossible dream. Perhaps a partner, close relation or friend may be able to offer help? Or a helpline, e.g. Beat UK, or a self-help group. Talking to other experienced carers or perhaps a professional, and discussing a way forward, can help with stress and isolation.

 REFLECTION POINTS

One of the key aims of treatment is to enhance the social connection and boost trust and security in relationships. Family members can play a large role in strengthening this atrophied system. This is the first step before connections with others can develop.

Notes

1. Research has shown that, when playing a computer game, people with EDs were noted to have much lower levels of angry/frustrated expressions. Additionally, when watching happy films or watching smiling babies, they failed to mirror and join in with these expressions of joy and happiness. Furthermore, when watching a sad film, not only was their facial expression flat but they turned away more. The expressionless poker face gives an impression that the individual is aloof or does not care. This lack of emotions on the outside contrasts with the intense internal emotions (often despair).
2. You might be interested to read work by Robert Dunbar, who has developed the social brain hypothesis. In essence, this is the idea that brain size is highly correlated with the size of social networks. Thus birds who pair bond have higher brain size than those who find a new mate each season.

11

Modelling emotional intelligence and problem-solving skills

People with eating disorders often find it difficult to manage and regulate emotions. They may try to avoid feeling, thinking about and acknowledging painful emotions, and sometimes act as if showing or talking about difficult emotions – such as hurt, anger and sorrow – is unacceptable. They may be unable to react verbally and actively at the appropriate time, to the appropriate person and at the appropriate level. In other words, they may have perfected the *art of avoidance*. At other times, their emotional output may be intense and extreme.

Events from conception onwards can sensitise the emotional system. Stressful experiences, perhaps even before birth and during development, can interfere with the development of a sense of safety, possibly leaving them more susceptible to emotional stress than many other people. And difficult experiences and constant hassles can overwhelm the ability of the family to manage emotional regulation – and may lead to an individual later developing an eating disorder with less mature emotional regulation strategies ... which can develop into a very tangled web indeed, for Edi's household, for family and often for close others.

Emotions are what make us human and guide our progress through life. The maturation of emotional intelligence is a key part of development. We discussed earlier how this developmental process can get derailed by an eating disorder and how starvation – leading to that tangled web – severely disrupts things (see Chapter 2).

Therefore, a key aspect of treatment is to learn – or perhaps relearn – how to manage emotions. Chapter 8, 'Communication', includes discussion as to how carers – who may recognise elements of, for instance, Kangaroo, Ostrich or Rhino, in their own behaviour – can model adaptive emotional processing for Edi. Carers may recognise that they too need to modify and change a particular response or behaviour. Through modification and effective demonstration, Edi can learn – or relearn – these skills.

Edi will need help in being able to master the difficulties and risks entailed in communicating negative emotions. Often people with eating disorders have a default tendency to be 'people pleasers' – leading to feeling that they are unable to control their own lives. Failure to be emotionally honest in a respectful way may lead to a build-up of hurt and anger, feeling useless because their unexpressed inner feelings are so intense and huge. To express such negative feelings may seem disgusting and out of control; and trying to suppress those difficult feelings – rather than discuss them when they arise – can lead to explosions of temper.

Often the only other outlet for extreme feelings may seem to Edi to be in forms of self-punishment, self-abuse, self-starvation, vomiting, laxatives, over-exercise, etc. Physical pain may be more acceptable than emotional pain. Sometimes self-control breaks and the result is bulimia, leading to further feelings of intense disgust, which again they may have difficulty in expressing directly.

An eating disorder can take hold because it comes to serve a function for a vulnerable individual, who finds that it helps control or dull strong emotions. Starvation may take the edge off the intensity of emotions, making the sufferer 'feel numb', allowing Edi to isolate and suppress the continuous bombardment of negative feelings. By restricting food intake and dulling emotions, sufferers remove themselves from the hurt, pain and perceived injustice in their lives – perhaps triggered by a broken relationship, a bereavement, moving house or school or job – with intense feelings of loss or leaving behind an important part of Edi's life.

Other eating-related behaviours such as bingeing, over-exercising and vomiting may also be a way of trying to soothe or distract from those intense feelings. Sometimes patients describe themselves as being 'full'. This fullness is felt as a physical sensation but, in reality, they are actually 'full' of feelings and emotions. Some sufferers deal with the 'fullness' by purging or vomiting, others are unable to eat – they feel enormous, like a balloon, taut and stretched by these intense and difficult feelings.

The tendency to avoid emotions happens automatically so that Edi may not even recognise that she or he feels an emotion, and may also be unaware that others might pick up on their non-verbal emotional reaction (a slight blush of the cheeks, a tear in the eye, hesitation in speech, turning away the head or casting down the eyes).

ACTION POINTS

 How to be an emotional coach

There are five basic steps to being an emotional coach for Edi: **Attend, Label, Validate, Regulate** and **Learning**.

1. **Look and listen for signs of negative emotions**, e.g. going quiet, eyes down, flushed, tears in eyes, micro-movements in eye, nose or mouth that register the flash of an emotion, or breaking flow of conversation. This is difficult as facial emotional expression is suppressed.

Show that you have attended to this – *'I see that you are upset; I notice that when I said … your eyes became downcast/you turned your head away. I noticed the tear in your eye … I can see by this that you are either upset or angry in some way. Can you try to tell me more about what you are feeling and thinking?'*

2. **Label** – *'I wonder if you are sad/angry/upset because…'* Encourage Edi to voice the difficulty. Do they feel hurt, disgust or anger? Ask Edi to talk about what they feel at the moment. *'What are you thinking?'*, *'Would it be helpful to talk about it a bit?'* or *'Might it be a good idea to reflect on it a little?'* Take the time to listen and try to understand the context. Guide Edi through the process of analysing what is going on. Sometimes talking about specific feelings and emotions is so alien to sufferers that, although they know they are feeling something, usually too much, they cannot describe exactly what.

If Edi finds it too hard to express their thoughts aloud, perhaps encourage them to express their feelings through writing or perhaps a drawing/artwork … Sometimes the suggestion of making up – and naming – a character then writing their feelings down in story form for that character can help Edi feel a little more detached and therefore more able to express those feelings.

3. **Validate** – with empathy. *'It looks to me as if…'*, *'I may be wrong but you seem…'*, *'You seem angry/sad/hurt.…'* *'Often when people have an expression like that they feel.…'*, *'I can understand why you might feel sad. You were really looking forward to getting off the ward. I can see you're disappointed. I might feel the same way.'*

This can then open up a conversation in which Edi may be able to acknowledge what they might need, how they may feel thwarted or rejected by others and/or how they experience conflict. The aim of the conversation is to approach rather than avoid difficulties – which is Edi's automatic tendency. Talking about personal experiences and especially difficulties increases Edi's ability to examine and master emotions and to understand the bigger picture about whether the emotion is signalling something important or whether perhaps Edi is oversensitive and possibly over-reacting.

Listen carefully to the painful thoughts; do not prematurely brush them off or reassure – it is shaming and humiliating to have your feelings and fears brushed aside (e.g. *'Don't be silly! Of course you don't need to be scared of that!'* or *'You are being ridiculous! You shouldn't get offended by things like that!'*). No matter how differently from Edi you may feel, try to put yourself in Edi's shoes. Try to understand what they are saying and to pick up the underlying message which the sufferer may have difficulty in expressing directly. *'You feel hurt because....', 'You feel angry because ...', 'You feel really upset about.... Am I right?'*

4. **Regulate** (soothing and redirecting emotions) – model good emotional regulation strategies. Give positive feedback about the ability to express an emotional response because this is a core step of emotional regulation. *'I am very impressed that you are able to tell me about your distressing feelings. Well done for having the courage to tell me you felt hurt/angry/sad.'*

Allow Edi to feel emotional pain sometimes. Don't have unrealistic expectations – for example, wanting Edi to be happy all the time (no one can be.) There must be balance between positive and negative emotions – that is the human condition. Positive and negative emotions are the accelerators and brakes guiding us through life and they make us who we are ... *'Let me give you a hug. And then let's plan to do something fun together.'*

Try not to over-identify with Edi's feelings, or get overwhelmed by your own reaction to what he or she might be feeling, i.e. their sadness or victory is not your sadness or victory. *Take a step back and remain the carer offering support and help when needed. Sometimes no words are needed – you can express support and a wish to help simply by, for example, giving a hug or sympathetic pat on the shoulder.*

Be grown up about any negative feedback you get – take it on the chin. Remember you need to model how every mistake can be a treasure. If you do not understand the particular feelings (because you do not share the sufferer's view of whatever event has caused a problem), perhaps you could say, *'Thank you for explaining how you see things. I'm sorry you feel that way and you feel upset/angry/sad. I see things differently and I'd like to explain how I feel about this…'* It is important not to over-react to Edi's emotion, i.e. try not to feel threatened by their anger, or defensive at their criticisms, hurt by separations, or rejected by their disinterest. Try to react calmly; take a break when needed. *'I'm tired right now, let's talk about this later.'* But, make sure that time is found to do just that – don't say or promise to do anything you can't follow through.

5. **Learning** – what does the emotion tell you that you might need?

An emotional reaction signals an unfulfilled need. Sometimes these needs can be addressed by problem solving and action strategies. However, sometimes it is important to *reset goals and use mindfulness and acceptance strategies to cope with the unfulfilled need.*

Emotional registration and sensitisation

Although Edi has difficulty naming and defining her or his own emotions, they may be highly attuned to the non-verbal emotions of others – especially associated with threat. Beware of telling 'white lies' – 'No, I am not upset' etc. – when you do indeed feel upset. If you deny your own emotional response, then you are modelling stifling and non-attending emotions.

For example, whilst walking out with their mother, Edi passed some old school friends. Edi said, 'You must feel embarrassed when people stare at me when we're out together.' What would be the best response to Edi's words?

An emotionally unintelligent response would be to say, 'No, of course I am not embarrassed by you. You look lovely' – which is a white lie as the mother is desperately worried about Edi's 10 kg weight loss.

Here are some examples of more emotionally intelligent responses:

> 'Do you feel ashamed about your illness when you see old friends?' (It may be the case that Edi has projected his or her own emotional response onto others.)
>
> 'I am not embarrassed, but I feel upset and worried that you lost weight last week after what you told me you would do.'

Relationship ruptures

Often people with an eating disorder have the tendency to assume that the world and people in it follow logical rules, keep to order, etc. However, in real life, unexpected and inexplicable events arise which may produce tensions and a feeling of being let down or misunderstood – which can lead to ruptures in the relationship. Exploring and discussing together the underpinning emotions and thoughts that caused the rupture can lead to stronger bonds and closer relationships in the long term.

Working to repair relationship ruptures (emotional scars)

The APT approach can be used to work through any past emotional problems

---

 Acknowledging past problems and expressing regret is a wonderful opportunity to model the skills which will be needed to sustain future relationships. Hindsight clarifies mistakes. But mistakes are opportunities to learn and become wiser for the future – therefore, every mistake is a treasure as it gives us experience to learn how better to tackle things for the future.

An *'if only!'* blaming mindset is harmful, whereas a compassionate mindset is helpful.

When the eating-disordered individual is young, difficult events are hard to process as the immature mind cannot see the bigger picture, and when Edi is older often their very mixed, complex emotions are equally hard to understand. With the right support, and carer resilience, Edi's painful past memories can be acknowledged and discussed – then re-embedded in a new context.

Cherishing the positive

In our work with families, we find a letter on the subject of *'What you mean to me'* leads to a new positive foundation for the relationship. Edi can have doubts about whether you love them as their sense of safety is less well developed, or has been badly affected by the illness – but these letters can help build this up.

Planning for these conversations is important. Writing notes or a letter can help you maintain a wider perspective. Here is a letter written by Rosemary, which may give you ideas:

> Dear Jane,
>
> I have been reviewing our life together and reflecting on my role as your mother. Our relationship did not get off to as good a start as I would have liked.
>
> As you know, my father was diagnosed with his brain tumour when I was pregnant with you and he died when you were six months old. I feel my own grief prevented me from being a good mind-reader and in tune with your needs, thoughts and emotions. You perhaps learned that if you showed distress it caused me pain and anxiety. I am sure I struggled to share your joy and pick up on what gave you pleasure. This may have made you more sensitive to stress. Perhaps you also failed to learn that you could be reliably soothed by others.
>
> I want to do my best to repair this relationship. I cannot promise that I will not get it wrong again. Nothing is more important to me than building a good relationship with you. I know that this will be a source of support and strength for both of us. So I want to start by asking forgiveness for not being able to give you the strong start in life that I would have liked to give you.

 Every situation is different. Another letter, from Grace:

> Dear Ellie,
>
> I want you to know how much I love you, always loved you since the day you were born. I can still picture that day in April, and the nurse said 'It's a girl, a lovely little girl'. I remember being in the ward and feeding you … so many lovely memories as you grew.
>
> I know that life has seemed very difficult over the last

couple of years and that all sorts of things have gone wrong for you. Bea was your best friend, you did so much together before she moved to work in London. Then starting your new job and working every day with Chris, who seems to be a very awkward character (also every day, from what you've told me!).

And now I know that your marriage has broken down … I'm so glad you felt able to tell me about E's temper and violence towards you. So glad that you felt able to return home here, glad that you have felt able to talk to some of your good friends and they've really helped you to get through.

And so glad that we can talk – and be honest with each other. I've said that I really don't like it when you shout at me (I think maybe you really want to shout at the world and all that's gone wrong for you, is that how you feel?) and it meant so much to me that, when you had calmed down, today you came and said sorry.

I can see how hard you are trying to beat your illness, 'anorexia binge/purge type' you said the doctor called it, and I feel so proud of all your efforts.

I've always loved you, dear Ellie, always will.

Mum xxx

REFLECTION POINTS

1. In this chapter, we have discussed the confusing emotional interactions caused by the heightened sensitivity to threat and inhibited facial displays of emotion that are part of the ill state of an eating disorder. We have discussed how you may need to make allowances for Edi's decreased social communication skills due to the illness.

2. Your role is to teach by example using adaptive and wise emotional regulation skills and communicating with warmth and compassion. This is not easy – but well worth the effort to help Edi towards recovery.

3. During your discussions with Edi, try to prepare beforehand for what may be a difficult topic. Work out what you want to say and use your own words to *gently point out to Edi that* 'Admission to hospital, – or restricted activities – may be needed to safeguard your health ...'

modelling emotional intelligence

12

Managing undereating

Introduction

Through this chapter, we hope to be able to guide you, and Edi, through the many challenges eating poses. We work through eating at different stages of the illness. Of course, not all this chapter may be relevant to you, or Edi, immediately. You may work forwards, and backwards, through the topics as the dynamics of Edi's illness change. If not all pertinent to you at the present, maybe the information contained here will aid your reflection on past progress made or offer hope and promise for future achievements.

The aim of treatment for an eating disorder is to return food and meals to their normal place – as fuel. Furthermore, as eating has a central role within all cultures, providing a backdrop for socialising, celebration and enjoyment, it is an important source of connection and shared pleasure. Reintegrating into life (work, school, relationships, friends, college, etc.) also involves reintegrating into food (birthday dinners, supper invitations, lunch meetings, cooking for friends, picnics, BBQs, etc.). Initially, 'food is fuel' in the treatment process but, later, and sometimes much later (sometimes years), the aim of treatment is to help the sufferer to see food again in the context of friends, family, talking and connecting. This is a tough assignment for any sufferer and frequently imagined as inconceivable and impossible.

Thus the goal of helping someone to recover from an eating disorder is to coach Edi to relearn how to:

1. eat sufficient for the body's needs

2. eat flexibly and with variety

3. eat socially – with food set into the context of the bigger picture of life.

A step-by-step approach is used to work towards these goals.

A The role of eating and eating behaviours

Eating is non-negotiable

All living creatures must eat to live – whether to eat or not is non-negotiable. The body has a variety of control systems in place to ensure that an individual does not die of starvation – nourishing all parts of the body and brain means eating is one of the basic needs of all living organisms.

Eating disorders, especially anorexia nervosa, where refusal is of every scrap of nourishment and sometimes of liquid too, disrupt one of the core aspects of living. However, although eating is a non-negotiable area, the How, Where, When, What and With Whom of food and eating *are* areas that can be negotiated.

As early weight restoration can lead to a shorter illness course, it is important to get on to 'change talk' as soon as possible. When the illness follows a long course, patterns and rituals become deeply ingrained and highly habitual. The longer the illness continues, the harder it is for Edi to contemplate change. 'Change talk' is therefore a priority; the sooner the better.

Carrots and sticks

We are all designed to be motivated to do things that are rewarded – for example, that give us pleasure or are 'nice' in some way – and to turn away from things that are not rewarded, in other words, nasty. One of the difficult things to understand is how this principle works in relation to an eating disorder. From the outside it is difficult to imagine how *not* eating could possibly be rewarding in any way. However, there seem to be some perceived positive benefits for people with an eating disorder, possibly because there is something unusual in the biological response to starvation or the meaning of not eating. It is as if starvation is somehow uplifting, vitalising and energising to sufferers. A number of secondary effects may also become rewarding or feel somehow pleasurable (for example, more personal attention, care, compliments). However, habits become disconnected to goals and become 'mindless' repetitive acts.

In treatment at the Maudsley, to explore these reasons, we ask people to write a letter to 'anorexia nervosa, the friend'. A questionnaire was developed and over 300 women with anorexia nervosa were surveyed to examine what were the most common negative and positive aspects of their eating disorder. We found that the most common rewards were:

- Anorexia makes me feel safe, secure and in control.

- Anorexia is a way of showing my distress.

- Anorexia is a way of helping me avoid growing up and what that entails – responsibility.

It is probable that some of these are relevant to your loved one. In order to help Edi change and leave any eating disorder behind, carers will need to help Edi to find other ways to get these rewards. For example:

- Find other ways of helping Edi feel safe, secure and in control. As outlined in previous chapters, one of the best ways of doing this is in an atmosphere in which there is *calmness, consistency, compassion* and *love* – not easy to create such an atmosphere when everyone is worried, anxious, on edge, walking on egg shells, which is common in families coping with an eating disorder.

- Find other ways of communicating and dealing with distress (coaching in emotional intelligence; Chapter 11).

- Find ways of making the experience of taking personal responsibility more positive (coaching to develop skills to face problems and seek solutions; to be more flexible; and to take in the bigger picture).

We have developed a model which attempts to explain how undereating *may* be maintained. In this model, eating and food (or secondary linked features such as weight and shape) become associated with added and unusual meaning and value for Edi. This meaning becomes embedded in the individual's identity, along with changes in informational processing (rigidity, and detailed analysis) and emotional systems (anxiety), which shape the consequent behaviours. This leads to rule-driven eating and avoidance. Eating is decontextualised and is not merely a behaviour used to satisfy hunger, supply essential nutrients or as part of social bonding. These rules about eating *may* relate to weight control but frequently they are far more complex – for example, whether Edi feels 'good enough' to eat or 'merits' the reward of eating food, whether they have worked hard enough or achieved enough to 'earn' a meal, whether they are 'worthy enough' to take up space. The rules may be idiosyncratic, involving some function of food, such as colour or aesthetics or the effect on sexuality or performance. Often 'rule-bound eating' has complex emotional undertones, which are personal, peculiar, often unfounded and directly related to food and meals.

A few examples of Edi's 'food rules':

> 'I can't eat this, it will make me fat.'
>
> 'I can't eat that because it is green.'
>
> 'If I eat my food in a clockwise order going round my plate, it makes me less anxious.'
>
> 'I have to chew each mouthful 15 times.'
>
> 'I must eat the vegetables on my plate first, then the protein, then the carbohydrate. Things cannot be mixed.'
>
> 'If I eat any oil my weight will shoot up immediately.'
>
> 'I can't eat this because it will poison me, it is red.'
>
> 'I haven't accomplished enough today to deserve dinner.'
>
> 'I must always leave a tiny bit on my plate – even if it's a single grain of rice, or one cornflake.'
>
> 'I do not deserve to eat because I didn't finish task A in the right time.'
>
> 'Any food that I do eat must be hot.'
>
> 'My exam mark should have been higher. I'm not good enough to eat.'
>
> 'Meals have to be on time: breakfast 8.00 a.m., lunch 12.30 p.m. and dinner 6.00 p.m. I won't eat them if they are late.'
>
> 'I can only eat X brand of yogurt.'
>
> 'I didn't accomplish my exercise regime today. Therefore I cannot eat.'

Perhaps you recognise a few of them – or perhaps your loved one has developed their own rigid food-related rules?

For Edi, following their individually developed rules about food and eating serves the function of reducing anxiety, at least in the short term. This is especially true for individuals who have developed an obsessive compulsive disposition valuing order and control, in those who have high levels of anxiety or those who are oversensitive to the reactions of others. Edi may also have an analytical eye for detail and reduce food to its elements, e.g. *how many calories, how much fat?* To change from this pattern of eating behaviour, an individual needs to zoom out and be able to see the bigger picture. This involves being able to step back to attain a broader perspective of meaning and value. *Compulsive, anxiety-laden thoughts about food have to be challenged, and it is necessary to work through and tolerate the high anxiety that this will inevitably produce. High anxiety will ebb away, especially if, as you provide support, you remain calm and do not get swept up in the emotion.*

Compensatory or 'safety behaviours'

At times Edi takes food to please and appease others, in response to powerful appetite cues (overwhelming hunger), or in an attempt to cover their disordered eating behaviour. This 'non-rule-bound' eating causes high anxiety.

When my daughter, aged 23, developed anorexia, binge/purge type, she ate a good healthy meal across the table from me each evening. I couldn't understand why she was losing weight – at the time I had never even heard the term 'an eating disorder'. (GLS)

I would hate the thought of friends seeing me as weak, pathetic or appearance conscious, the usual eating disorder stereotypes. If ever I had to eat with people I would restrict rigorously before-hand. I would then attempt to eat as normally as possible at dinner and conceal my terror. Panic-stricken after a 'huge' meal, I would walk home (miles) and exercise and restrict the next day to compensate for my 'indulgence'. (AC)

To cope with this distress, a variety of what are called 'safety' behaviours may develop – including vomiting, misuse of laxatives, over-exercising – or thoughts to try to neutralise the distress which are found soothing, such as: *'Once I am free I will choose how I will eat'*, or perhaps, *'Being made to eat doesn't count'*, etc.

> After she had eaten with me, she went upstairs to her bedroom, saying she wanted to watch TV. On the way to her bedroom she visited the bathroom to get rid of everything she had eaten. It was a long time before I realised what was happening. (GLS)

> Later on in my illness, although I still wouldn't feed myself adequately, I started to accept food from my parents. Giving food to myself was too indulgent; I was worthless and undeserving. Accepting food from others was different – the choice was removed and the guilt after eating was alleviated slightly. (AC)

As they reduce the anxiety caused by eating, these 'safety' behaviours can quickly become reinforced and habitual.

At times, Edi may involve other people to elicit reassurance. For example:

Edi: *'If I eat that I will get fat.'*
Response: *'Of course you won't.'*

A repetitive cycle can be set up with the carer providing the safety routine. These exchanges allow Edi to rehearse eating-disordered thinking, thereby reinforcing it. Ideally carers try to sidestep being invited to join in this dance.

> Response: *'I think you know that we all need food to live. The hospital has told me that I should not provide mindless reassurance so I will not say more.'*

New habits for health

The aim of treatment is to set the scene so that *the person with an eating disorder develops the skills and motivation to change*, to relax their rule-bound eating and put aside their safety.

Learning and memory are active processes involving brain growth and nerve synapse sprouting. Malnutrition produces a reduction in brain growth factors and interferes with learning and active brain function. Thus, a vicious circle develops: Starvation interferes with the function of the 'social brain' and maturation of cognitive functioning. The result is that social, emotional and intellectual functions are stunted. The capacity to reflect and the ability to step back and get an overview of emotions, thoughts and behaviours, all of which are essential to recovery, are impaired. And another trap is sprung.

Edi seems to regress to a much earlier level of development.

> When she was 23, at very low weight and very ill, my daughter frequently behaved as if she was about 3, with understanding and perceptions of around that age. (GLS)

> Your decision-making skills disappear. You have to ask for advice, reassurance and permission for everything. You can't interpret other people's reactions or emotions without guidance. You become totally dependent on others to function day-to-day, not just for nourishment, but to live. (AC)

Although it can be used for short periods to preserve life and improve brain function, forced feeding, and attempts to change the eating-disordered behaviour by coercion alone, will not lead to permanent change. Indeed coercion can lay down more food/fear memories.

Unless these restricted, rule-bound patterns of eating are modified, they can become habitual and hardwired into the brain.

Therefore, helping someone with an eating disorder involves a balancing act: on the one hand, giving the support needed to help develop motivation to explore and experiment with non-rule-bound eating and reduced safety behaviours; on the other hand, not letting malnutrition and eating disorder symptoms interfere with brain function by causing brain cell death, disrupting reward pathways, and inhibiting learning and development.

Summary

Overcoming eating disorder habits is hard as they become automatic and overlaid with high levels of emotion and thoughts that serve to embed them more deeply. The problem is that another illness spiral is sprung with illness eating habits being associated with high levels of anxiety for Edi. Next, close others see the signs of the illness and starvation and become terrified themselves. This high anxiety on both sides can lead to meals becoming a battle ground (research has shown this also occurs in eating disorder units). Memories of eating and stress become further embedded and embellished, the anxiety level at the next meal is ratcheted up a notch ... and so it goes on. You can break out of this spiral by managing your own anxiety and setting the environment so that meals are associated with calmness and care. A tough job but essential.

The body fights back – the bulimic trap

Extreme tension develops between rule-bound eating and the physiological cues that control appetite. The body and brain desperately need nourishment to function effectively, and a series of mechanisms to increase appetite fight against malnutrition caused by the starvation. The strength of these innate mechanisms varies between individuals. It is possible that some individuals, genetically predisposed to anorexia nervosa, have a more loosely regulated system. The lifetime memory bank and experience of food, eating and appetite are lost if abnormal eating behaviours persist for any length of time. Thus, the basic concepts of hunger and fullness have to be relearned and gradually trained to take over normal appetite control.

In some individuals the 'reward pathways' become so sensitive that, once eating restarts, it takes a while to shut off. A drive to overeat, with intense urges and cravings, may emerge.

Discuss Box 11.1 with Edi, and also the real-life stories of GLS and AC quoted on p. 127; encourage Edi to read other real-life stories in this book, e.g. Frances' story on p. 202.

A variety of perverse eating behaviours arise when rule-bound eating is at war with the biology of appetite, e.g. stealing foods and binge eating. The response to this drive, and the intense urges and cravings, will vary with the individual. For instance, in the restrictive type of AN, purging behaviours such as vomiting may not be part of the scene, while in AN binge/purge type it may enter the picture at an early or later stage. Chapter 13 focuses on helping to reduce bingeing and over-eating behaviours.

B Thinking about changing bad eating habits

Insight using the nutritional risk ruler

In Chapter 7, the use of a 'Readiness Ruler' to aid motivation to change is illustrated. Here, we use the same tool to discuss the balance between motivation to change and objective evidence of nutritional safety. The 'Nutritional Risk Ruler' gauges Edi's insight into the potential impact the illness has on their medical health as well as their quality of life, in both the short and the long terms. *The aim is to initiate a conversation discussing nutritional health.*

Use the Nutritional Risk Ruler to discuss with Edi the risks to the others with an eating disorder.eg 'What would you say to your friend with an eating disorder? What would you say to their families?'

Talking about the stories/experiences of other people with eating disorders, asking 'Is this how you feel?', can lead to more detached thinking about the long-term effects of e.g. severe diet restriction; bingeing and purging. Asking Edi 'Is this how you feel?' may trigger questioning thoughts for Edi about his/her own condition and situation.

Nutritional risk ruler

> *Ability to ensure nutritional safety and maintain full nutritional health*
>
> *0——1——2——3——4——5——6——7——8——9——10*

ACTION POINT

Plotting nutritional risk

1. Using the Ruler, start by asking how Edi would rate their current ability to manage their own nutritional well-being. Mark this on the Ruler.

2. Follow up this score with reflections and further questions. For example:

   - *Why that score?*

   - *Why that score rather than 0?* (This can often elicit motivational statements as it asks for thoughts and behaviours that are in a positive change direction.)

   - *What would have to happen for you to be at 7?*

   - *What help would be needed to help you get to 7 or 10?*

   Here, you are setting the scene for, and encouraging, 'change' talk.

3. Edi may give themselves a high score, at variance with your judgement. If this occurs, ask whether you can illustrate *your* position using the same tool. *'Would you mind if I use the same Ruler to mark where it seems you are from my perspective?'*

4. Explain calmly, with observations and feedback, why you have given that score:

   - *'I would put you on a 4 because I see that you are very sensitive to the cold – when I go up to your room you have extra heat on, which is one of the signs of malnutrition.'*

   - *'The doctor told us that your blood pressure and pulse rate are very low.'*

   - *'The examination came up red on some of the risk factors on his chart.'*

   Avoid sounding critical or judgemental. Use first-person observations: *'I notice….'*, or third-person statements: *'The doctor says…'*.

   Avoid *'You this or that…'*, which sound accusatory.

   Or:

   - *'I notice that you have given yourself a higher score than I have been able to do. What do you think you would be able to do to show me that I am being too pessimistic? How could you show me that you can take care of yourself and that your score is higher?'*

5. Given any discrepancy between objective and subjective scores, ask Edi how much others (including yourself) will be needed to safeguard their health.

- *'It is up to you how you manage your nutritional health. You are the only one who can decide this.'* Whenever possible, emphasise Edi's freedom and ability to choose. This helps increase motivation.

6. As well as emphasising choice, highlight that your help is available when she or he is ready.

- *'If there is anything I can do to help you improve your nutritional health, then please say. I am more than happy to assist and support you in any way that I can – both practically and emotionally. I trust that when you would like help, you will ask me. The offer is always open.'*

Society's responsibility for nutritional safety

Ideally, enough time will be available to gently raise awareness with Edi of the consequences, to life and health, of inadequate nourishment. Ideally, enough time will be available to work towards motivating Edi to think about, initiate and maintain changing eating behaviour. Ideally, enough time will be available to raise Edi's self-esteem and confidence that he or she can succeed through all setbacks encountered. However, unfortunately there are situations – for instance, when an individual's current medical state is perilous or highly unstable – when the necessary time or resources are not available at home.

ACTION POINT

Plotting medical risk

You may want to look at standard growth and development charts: www.cdc.gov

A BMI of below 13.5 kg/m^2 is a marker of high medical risk, and inpatient treatment is recommended. If risk is in these areas, doctors and lawyers consider using the Mental Health Act (MHA; see Chapter 3) to ensure safety. The possibility of using the MHA needs to be discussed with Edi in addition to the dangers and mortality risk at this low weight. It is reasonable to open a discussion about this as, unfortunately, anorexia nervosa has the highest mortality rate of any psychiatric disorder. Both professional and lay carers should discuss the necessity of using the MHA in a non-personalised way. It is a care pathway that has to be followed when needed, as part of good practice, and is not used to bully or threaten. As always, gentle persuasion using motivation through discussion is preferable to confrontation and admission to hospital completely against Edi's wishes. Although, when there is high risk, eating becomes the top priority.

A BMI of 16 kg/m^2 is considered to be a severe degree of malnutrition by the World Health Organization.

Some sufferers, now in recovery, have commented that discussions around such charts had not been helpful to them at the time of their illness. They have reflected that visualising their position on the chart provided them with yet more motivation to lose weight to be considered in a lower BMI category or as 'severely malnourished' etc. As a carer, independently plotting BMI so you are aware of the situation and then engaging Edi in general conversations about medical risk and consequences may be more helpful. Using the 'Nutritional Risk Ruler' task, calmly explain the situation to Edi. Here is an example:

- *'It looks as if it is difficult for you to be aware of your own nutritional health. If we put in some of the objective*

*observations about your body function there are
indications that your health/growth and development
are in jeopardy. Yet you are unable to feel this. The
evidence for this is the large discrepancy between your
score and mine on the Nutritional Risk Ruler. Look – your
score is here, but I've marked mine here. It looks as if you
are being tricked by the eating disorder into thinking that
there is nothing wrong and that you are OK. That is not
the case. I am very worried, and need extra help.'*

As before, find your own words to talk with Edi about the
effects of his or her illness on Edi's health.

Your responsibility to safeguard Edi's well-being needs to
be calmly explained. Remember the St Bernard dog
behaviour.

ACTION POINT

Explaining society's role to Edi

*'If your illness means that you cannot be responsible for
your nutritional health, then I have a duty of care to safeguard
your life. In court I would be considered responsible for your
health, and negligent if I just stood by and did nothing.'*

*'Society also holds itself responsible for safeguarding
nutritional health in people with eating disorders. That's why
there are statutory rules such as the Mental Health Act – do
you remember what the MHA means?.'*

*'If we use this line to represent the degree of responsibility
that society needs to take for your health, where do think you
are on this line?'*

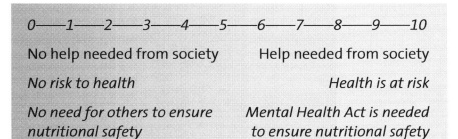

0——1——2——3——4——5——6——7——8——9——10

No help needed from society   Help needed from society

No risk to health   *Health is at risk*

No need for others to ensure *Mental Health Act is needed*
nutritional safety   *to ensure nutritional safety*

'Why that score rather than 7?'

'What would have to happen for you to be at 1?'

'What help will you need until you can get to 1?'

If the eating disorder is severe it will be difficult for Edi to have a realistic perspective. The conversation may go like this:

'You have told me that you do not think you need help and that you can care for your nutritional safety. I understand that is how it "feels" to you. However that's in contrast to the objective facts. Let us try to think of the least restrictive way we can work within the rules set down by society. I would prefer us to succeed at home rather than go to hospital. I would prefer it if you could make the plan. What help might you need from me to do that? What other help might you need?'

C Creating distance from eating disorder rules

The following section illustrates the type of processes used in therapy to increase the motivation to move away from rule-bound eating. It may be helpful for you to be mindful of these and to experiment with using this sort of approach.

1 Distance through conversation

In order to foster change, it is necessary to build a non-eating disorder identity. The goal is to develop a range of more flexible, adaptive perspectives. The first stage in progress is to understand ambivalence, or feeling unsure and 'being in two minds'.

- What are the pros and cons of the status quo?

- What are the pros and cons about trying to change?

- What are the pros and cons of having a non-eating disorder identity and lifestyle?

Such a conversation might go like this:

> 'After getting into such a habit and routine with your pattern of eating, you must be terrified about how you will be able to break this pattern of behaving.'
>
> 'Your appetite system may be disrupted by the eating disorder. The effort needed to relearn how to regain normal nutritional health will be immense; maybe you think it would be too difficult for you?'

> - This reflection over-emphasises the difficulty of change. The therapist is speaking in the role of a 'Devil's Advocate', indicating how very difficult change might be. The natural reaction to such a stance is for the person with the eating disorder to come back with a reply from the opposite point of view, i.e. to state that it might not be so bad, Edi may be able to do something positive to preserve their health...

The following is the type of reply you sometimes elicit from Edi (though perhaps not in these words).

> *'No, I am not terrified that I can't do it because I've made some changes already. For example, I used to use food either to punish or to reward myself. I'd only allow myself to eat depending on how I judged the day had gone. Now I'm able to make sure I can eat no matter what the day has been like. Also, I found it difficult to eat because my judgement of hunger was unreliable. In the past I would always choose a non-calorific drink but now I am replacing these with yogurt drinks or smoothies to increase my calorie intake. I've learnt that my signals of hunger and my feelings trick me.'*

The 'Devil's Advocate' stance may also be used to examine what is positive for Edi about their illness, and simultaneously raise questions in Edi's mind.

> *'There must be things that you find positive about poor nutritional health, or would be afraid to lose, if you tried to attain better nutritional health?'*

- The aim of these questions is to develop awareness of discrepancy and dissonance. Challenging the eating disorder in this way brings with it some sort of distress – which may be expressed in a variety of individual ways – *but this emotional charge, whether through explosive rages, screaming or roaring, is essential for motivation.*

By building up discrepancy such a conversation sets the negative aspects of the illness against the positive aspects seen by Edi. It is helpful if you can listen to those aspects of the eating disorder seen as positive by Edi. Beware of prematurely stepping in; rubbishing and invalidating what is said. Thoroughly explore what is meant so that you can see whether there are other ways in which Edi can attain his or her illness's perceived benefits.

Box 12.1 amalgamates thoughts expressed by many eating disorder sufferers; the pros (reasons as to why a sufferer may be reluctant to give up their illness) and the cons (negative, dismissive feelings towards the eating disorder). After reading the examples, maybe you will be able to appreciate how some of the comments are relevant to Edi.

BOX 12.1 Edi's thoughts about eating disorder

Reasons to stay with the eating disorder

- *Makes people listen to me.*

- *Makes me feel that people are concerned about me.*

- *I am cared for and looked after. Everything feels so safe.*

- *I get to spend more time at home with Mum and Dad. I don't have to do grown-up things like go to university or move away from home.*

- *Sense of achievement/satisfaction from holding off eating.*

- *Food is a treat: (a) at the end of the day – save up for dinner time; (b) unusual foods seem too indulgent; (c) thought of it helps to pass the time.*

- *I actually like a lot of the things I eat now and feel annoyed if I 'make myself' eat different things. Also feel bewildered by choice in supermarkets, so it's easier to go with what I know.*

- *Sense of gluttony if I eat more.*

- *The guilty feelings and sense of failure I have after I have over-indulged are just too terrible.*

- *Makes me feel different/special.*

- *Gives me influence over others.*

- *Fear of adult relationships and responsibilities.*

- *Males might find me attractive if I put on weight and look 'normal'. I don't want that. Anorexia is my defence mechanism. I want to look like I do now.*

- *Fear that I'll get better and nothing will have changed and the old dissatisfactions, injustices and problems will still be there, waiting for me.*

- *Feel I have sunk so low there's not much worse.*

- *It was a secret before but everyone knows now so what's the point in trying?*

- *It fills up all my thoughts and takes all my energy. If I give up the illness, my life will be empty. I'll have nothing.*

- *Worry that my worst fears will be realised – i.e. proof that if I do start enjoying eating and drinking again, and put on weight, I won't be able to continue once I reach a normal weight and will have to cut everything out again – it's easier just to never get used to it as I no longer miss most things.*

- *It's what I'm used to now – can't imagine anything different.*

- *My eating disorder has taken me out of life for so long. Compared to everyone else my age, I'm so young. I have lost too many years to catch up on now. It's too daunting.*

- *Fear of setting a precedent and raising others' expectations. People will expect me to do 'normal' things like socialise and have a boyfriend. This terrifies me.*

- *Everyone will notice my weight gain and then I will feel under pressure to achieve recovery. What if I then fail? People will watch me and talk about it – this will make eating in public very difficult.*

Reasons to move away from an eating disorder

- *I've lost so many friends through my illness. I've driven away my family too.*
- *The illness makes me selfish – I don't have the time or brain space to think about or care for others.*
- *I will not be able to have a family of my own if I stay with my anorexia.*
- *I've lost my freedom. I'm not allowed to do anything or go anywhere by myself. Everyone watches my every movement. No one gives me any privacy.*
- *I've missed out on so much because of my illness – holidays, birthdays, parties, Christmas, etc.*
- *The illness makes me lie and deceive people. I become a horrible person when it's with me.*
- *I will never be able to achieve my dream job as a vet unless I give up my eating disorder.*
- *I'm not allowed to do the things I love any more – like swimming and cross-country running.*
- *My bones are already thin. I am liable to develop osteoporosis at a young age.*

Encouraging Edi to discuss openly his or her beliefs as to the possible benefits and 'pitfalls' of their illness is a useful exercise. However, you may be disappointed – Edi will always be 'in two minds' about change…

'I am terrified about osteoporosis.' But then she or he may say, *'I do not want to gain any weight.'*

Or, *'The disability caused to me by spraining my ankle made me think of what it could be like to be immobilised with osteoporosis.'* But then, *'I see those people who have recovered from anorexia as fat.'*

These mixed messages and confusing thoughts can be difficult to tolerate. Carers may be tempted to step in to cover up, reach a conclusion and somehow make things easier for the sufferer. Try to avoid stepping in to reassure. Instead, validate how confusing it must be.

> *'I imagine it must be confusing or frustrating on the one hand, feel that you don't want to have physical health problems from your eating disorder, and on the other hand feel terrified of gaining weight.'*
>
> *'I can see that it must be very confusing and tiring for you to be able to think of your future and your ambitions when food is not around but when it comes to eating, all you can see is calories and fat and the detail on the plate.'*

For Edi, this is an uncertain and distressing time; once adamant, now intermittently doubtful, that their illness is of benefit. Edi's feelings will swing rapidly; they may have periods where positivity, looking to the future and scathing comments about the eating disorder shine through. Then will come the 'negative cloud'; arguments about meal size, comments about excessive fat, low self-esteem, despair, etc. The change can be rapid – literally minutes. They are in turmoil. This can be extremely frustrating for carers – try to keep in mind that, for Edi, the questioning and uncertainty caused by intense thoughts and feelings about the pros and cons about eating/not eating, will eventually help promote change.

I would sometimes have a really positive conversation with my Mum about the future, my plans, holidays, how I could get through the illness, my desire to give it up, etc. Then, it would be time for a meal or a snack. My world narrowed – I wouldn't be able to see past the calories and the image of me ballooning. My brain whirred with plans as to how I was

going to get rid of the food afterwards, how would I compensate? It would be so frustrating; the sudden snap change
– I had just been thinking so positively. Everything had
seemed possible, what happened? (AC)

2 Distance through ABC

ABC (Antecedents, Behaviour and Consequences) is an important
theoretical tool used in psychology to understand behaviour. To
change any behaviour, it is essential to consider **Antecedents**, i.e.
the triggers, or the internal and external setting conditions, that
promote the **Behaviour**, and the **Consequences** of the behaviour:
what positive internal or external effects follow from the
behaviour, or what punishing effects are averted or avoided. The
theory is that behaviour is triggered by events, and that humans
continue with behaviours that produce some sort of reward,
whether towards reaching a goal, or gaining personal attention.

Reading the list in Box 12.1 'Reasons to Stay With the Eating
Disorder', is it possible to work out what the **As** are to make
people want to follow eating disorder rules? These are a few –
you may think of more:

TABLE 12.1   Functional analysis of undereating

Antecedents	Consequences
Internal triggers	**Positive effects**
• Fear	• Special skill
• Rejected	• Control
• Emotional upset	• Concern from others
• Adverse food-related memories	• Emotional avoidance/suppression
External triggers	**Negative effects**
• 'Fat' talk	• Resentment from others
• Isolation/loneliness/rejection	• Consequences of starvation
• Criticism/hostility	

- Emotional triggers: feeling unworthy, unhappy, inadequate and anxious.

- Thinking triggers: thoughts in which food has additional or unusual meaning.

Changing the antecedents

By ensuring the atmosphere at home is as warm as possible, carers can promote positive conditions in the home or community that foster eating. Criticism and hostility only serve to increase anxiety, which makes eating difficult. *No matter how frustrating mealtime behaviour is*, remain calm – if you get anxious or angry, Edi becomes even more anxious and angry, and finds it more difficult to eat. Edi will use her anger/anxiety as an excuse to leave the table and refuse food.

Therefore, set the scene so that social eating can be as pleasant as possible; perhaps think beforehand of neutral topics to discuss at the table (e.g. current films at the cinema, last night's best programme on TV or sports news) or tell the family about your day or encourage another family member to speak of their activities. No matter how mundane the chat is, it will act as calming background noise for Edi.

If an uncomfortable or tense silence develops, think about having some low-volume tranquil music playing in the background before you all sit to start the meal. As a distraction, maybe instruct one family member to read out crossword clues, for example, or talk about activities planned for after the meal or at the weekend.

If you have time and energy, go the extra mile for attractive table settings or maybe eat outside if the weather is fine.

To overcome the eating-disorder-thinking triggers, assertiveness skills are needed. These include:

- **Being calm**. Be clear and firm when stating what you want to see happen and reminding Edi what has been agreed.

- **Being compassionate**. Acknowledge how difficult it is for Edi, with food in front of them, to see any other perspective and to want to change their eating habits. However, remind them that your perspective differs. Be prepared to repeat patiently what you want to happen.

- **Being caring and concerned**. Offer to help the other person in any way you can. Ask what Edi thinks might help.

- **Coaching**. Talk Edi through how their mind focuses on micro-detail and 'the now'. Explain that, as an observer, you are able to see the bigger picture and the future. Entering into a discussion about the detail of the diet is not helpful. People need to eat to live. You are interested in promoting life quality. That is your bottom line. You may need to repeat this message calmly, kindly – and persistently.

- **Not colluding**. Do not get drawn into reassurance-giving, e.g. questions such as *'This will make me fat, won't it?'* Try to keep to neutral discussion topics – perhaps try to think beforehand of some local news or events to talk about – and do not join in eating disorder talk about food, weight or shape.

Calm, coaching comments to keep the eating pace going are helpful:

'It is not helpful if you focus on the detail of what sort/what calories/what amount…'

'Let's stick to the plan – we are interested in nutrition for health and quality of life. We all have to eat to live.'

'What is more helpful is to keep your eye on what we want to achieve in terms of your life story. Let's talk about …' (e.g. what Edi would like to do in the holidays).

'I would like your life to be more than eating.'

'Rather than being stuck on nutritional basics, let's zoom out to connections to people and the world – what film would you like to see at the weekend? Or maybe we could go and see…?'

'I know that there is more to you than food and weight. Let's move on and get there.'

Changing the consequences

Both internal and external consequences need to be considered.

Internal consequences: Extreme anxiety is the commonest consequence for Edi when his or her individual eating disorder rules are not obeyed. A pattern of compulsive safety behaviours may develop after eating anything at all. As outlined earlier, these include: exercising, vomiting, purging, reassurance-seeking and calculating eating-disordered thoughts (i.e. plans to cut back later).

Helping Edi to master the intense surge of anxiety which occurs with the sensation of fullness *without* using one of these strategies is a core part of the process. Therefore, when helping to coach Edi into improving their nutritional health, remember it does not stop when the meal is over. Planning follow-up distracting activities can be helpful. A joint conversation, jigsaw puzzle, crossword, looking through a book or photo album, a gentle walk round the garden or up the road, or watching a brief news update, film or television programme are some of the things that can interrupt these compulsions.

Such a distraction should ideally last for about 30 minutes after a meal (15 minutes after a snack). After this period of time, Edi will feel less physically full and thus will be more unlikely to initiate a compensatory safety behaviour. Some sufferers may be too tense, angry and resentful after a meal to concentrate or participate in a joint activity. This fury may stem from eating but also from your presence preventing them from performing their planned safety behaviour. Edi may, and probably will, direct their rage onto you. Maybe try and encourage them to release their frustrations some other way – punching a pillow or a cushion, or drawing, painting or writing about how they feel. A post-meal food diary may help Edi to express their hatred and dissatisfaction with themselves and their life through words. How did that meal make them feel and why? Remember that many, if not all, eating disorder sufferers lack emotional intelligence and identifying and vocalising feelings presents a considerable challenge.

> *'I would like to help you through this tough, post-meal, anxiety. I know how agonising it is for you to resist your compulsive drive to … Remember that we set a goal of staying with the challenge for 30 minutes. How can I help? Shall we walk round the block and you can tell me about your day?'*
>
> *'I can see how distressed that meal has made you feel. I know you are angry and anxious. Maybe if you cannot explain or talk to me about your inner thoughts, then you could write them down? Just getting them out, somehow, may help you to feel less full physically by lifting some of the emotional burden you are currently carrying.'*

External consequences: It is important that rule-driven eating is not praised or seen as appropriate.

The following example may help to illustrate this by describing how to analyse 'rewarding' or 'non-rewarding' responses to Edi's behaviours:

> *Tania's mother, Sue, would sit with Tania throughout a meal and ensure that she had finished.*

(This is a good example of giving attention to the behaviour of the normal part of her daughter – the part that knows that it is necessary to eat to live.)

> *After the meal, Tania would retreat to her room in floods of tears. Sue would follow her daughter and hug her and try to comfort her.*

(This might be seen as rewarding and/or reinforcing anorexic behaviour by giving it attention – it is the 'anorexic minx' that is distressed by eating, not the normal part.)

> *Sue and her husband David analysed the situation. They decided that Sue should ignore the post-meal tears. They decided to approach Tania when she was in a calm state at their next meeting and offer to spend some time together after a meal to help distract her from her distress – for example, a walk around the block, watching a TV programme, etc.*
>
> *From then on, after the meal Sue reminded Tania that they were going to have a walk. Sue noticed that Tania's tears did not last for very long if she ignored them. She also noticed that Tania gradually opened up more during their time together.*

Remember that these kinds of rewards, such as your attention and care, are the most potent motivators. For example:

> 'When we finish this meal, let's do more of the collage/weaving/scrapbook together.'
>
> 'When you finish this, let's go for a walk together.'
>
> 'It is tough to pull away from pain, but let's try to put it away for now. Imagine it in your big toe for now while you and I play Scrabble/watch that programme...'
>
> Or ..?

(Through discussion, each family will find different solutions and ideas depending on the individuals involved.)

D Implementing eating

Choices

There is no choice about whether to eat or not. However, choice can be given about *where* to eat a meal or snack: '*Would you prefer to have a snack in the garden or inside? Or, what about taking a picnic out for lunch?*' Within boundaries, *when* to eat can also be flexible: '*Would you prefer to have a snack at 3 or 4 o'clock?*' And, so can *with whom*. Additionally, Edi has yet another choice: *what* to eat (note – *what* rather than *if* to eat). Suggest two or three alternatives: '*Would you prefer a yogurt, toast or a smoothie for a snack?*'

Working to change rule-bound eating behaviour

It is important that families work together on issues related to eating. This is not easy as different personality styles can favour contrasting approaches. Also, some family members may have their own issues around food, clouding matters further. With so much media focus on body image, shape, weight and 'healthy eating', many people regularly follow diets or 'watch what they eat'. It is more difficult to take a non-biased perspective if any family member holds extreme shape and weight concerns. Additionally, supermarket food packaging and branding is geared towards the 'calorie conscious' – *'only 100 calories per bar!'*, *'reduced fat!'*, *'99 per cent fat free'*. Such clearly labelled food items are unhelpful to have in kitchen cupboards when Edi is around and are certainly not suitable for a weight-increasing diet. A family discussion and joint decision needs to take place about where such products should be kept and whether labels should be stuck over the nutritional information on these foods, etc. Additionally, discussion needs to focus on the eating behaviours of other family members. Maybe someone else other than Edi has a behaviour that requires challenging? It is difficult as there is a fuzzy line between what counts as an eating disorder symptom and what is 'normal' eating behaviour. However, an eating disorder thrives on splits and divides within a family, so what is important is a consistent, joint family approach.

Planning

Once Edi has resolved mixed feelings about change and has reached the stage of Action (see Chapter 7), you can then help and support in making detailed implementation plans.

Remember, Edi should have been aware before reaching this stage that your support and help was, and will be, always available. She or he may not have been ready for it previously, but on reaching the stage of Action you can start planning and discussing putting change into place *together*. It is important to bear in mind that setbacks are often encountered as commitment to change and energy fluctuate. At times, the eating disorder may be renewed, with a return to an earlier stage of the illness (see Chapter 7), so be prepared for this.

1 Planning – Discussion time

For Edi, eating involves the skill set of fighting fears. This means setting a hierarchy of goals, grading the degree of anxiety for each one, and then going through them sequentially, starting from the least anxiety provoking, and not moving to the next step until the expected anxiety settles down. Table 12.2 shows an example of a hierarchy grid.

TABLE 12.2   A hierarchy grid

Goal	Expected anxiety (0–100)	Actual anxiety (0–100)
Eating in a restaurant	99	
Going for a coffee and cake with friends	90	
Going for a cup of tea with sister	85	
Eating dinner with the family and aunt	75	
Eating a sandwich with family	65	
Eating fruit with family	60	

Key points

- Tackle one problem at a time.
- Break down tougher problems into steps.
- Start with a behaviour that is more manageable.
- Imagine walking through the plan in detail. Pre-practise tricky steps if possible through discussion with a family member or close friend.
- Observe the anxiety; remember that it is normal and beneficial response in the right circumstance, but it needs rewiring.
- If Edi takes over again, and refuses to eat what is planned, reflect every mistake is treasure: maybe the goal you set up for yourself is too challenging maybe better to start with something easier. Maybe you could do with support… Ask! *Don't give up, you will eventually succeed.*

- If you succeed, and follow through on your plan, then go on to tackle your next challenge.

It is important to go through this planning stage in great detail. Edi needs to feel safe and secure with when, and how, eating plans are to be implemented. Trying to challenge or change too much too soon will cause Edi to return. Remember, to the sufferer, you are 'trifling' with their safety blanket and 'messing' with their emotional crutch and dearest confidante. Concrete eating plans are particularly important when medical risk is high and treatment is stuck. Given Edi's state of health, you may have grand plans, but Edi certainly will not.

The overall aim is to help and support Edi to get to a healthy weight. Scientific evidence indicates that for recovery to occur, it is essential for people to return to the normal weight range. This has been put into the Clinical Guidelines for good practice in the management of anorexia nervosa. The aim is a BMI of between $19.5 \, kg/m^2$ and $25 \, kg/m^2$. This is because it:

- reduces the relapse risk

- lowers the risk of short- and long-term complications

- lowers the risk of onset binge eating

- reduces the alteration in brain chemistry that causes impulsive behaviours, self-harm, etc.

- reduces the alteration in brain chemistry that causes competitive, aggressive behaviours, irritability, etc.

- reduces the alteration in brain chemistry that causes over-activity etc.

In anorexia, without weight gain, it may be impossible for Edi to refrain from eating disorder-linked behaviours (social isolation, difficulty with emotional processing, and rigid and sad thinking). If Edi continues to play by eating disorder rules rather than reaching a state of normal physiology and biology, they will remain trapped within the abnormal processes that happen when people are starving and stressed.

Progress may be slow. You know you are starting to make progress once Edi's hands and feet are warmer. The following text gives you some pointers of how and what to discuss when planning with Edi.

(a) Naming and shaming rules: Ask Edi to walk you through what it would be like for a full day in his or her life if she or he were to take more responsibility for his or her own nutritional health. Additionally, introduce the concept of gradually loosening, through 'naming and shaming', any eating disorder-bound rules Edi religiously follows (see p. 167 of this chapter for examples). Edi will probably be reluctant to discuss these rules – being of a highly personal nature. Additionally, Edi will be acutely conscious of ridicule and embarrassment and sceptical of any benefit disclosure may bring. Encourage Edi by emphasising the 'naming and shaming' aspect of the exercise. Remind him or her that you can be there to offer support throughout Edi's actions when breaking the rule/ritual and the consequent anxiety.

Here is how the conversation might go:

> *'Now I want you to walk me through what a day in your life would be like with you taking more responsibility for your health. I want you to go through it as if you're constructing a story board for a film with every action visualised in your mind and talked through in plans with me. Let's start with getting up ... Let's move on to breakfast.'*
>
> *'People with an eating disorder usually have lots of rules about eating. Can you tell me about any rules you might have?'*
>
> *'It will be terrifying for you to shift any of those rules. Which will we tackle first? Which would be the least overwhelming to try to break?'*

You could then have a discussion about how these rules could be gradually shifted. It may be helpful to rank the rules and work on breaking the minor ones at first, going on to the major ones later.

(b) Targeting safety behaviours: It may also be helpful to encourage conversation about safety behaviours (p. 168 of this chapter), i.e. the soothing strategies or neutralising thoughts used to calm and reassure Edi if they have been forced to eat because of social cues – for example, to please you. Your aim would be to help them modify these thoughts into something more adaptive.

> *'You probably have your own way of soothing yourself if you feel forced to break your own rules by someone else. Can you please tell me how you manage this?'*
>
> *'It is a common problem to be so focused on detail that you cannot see the bigger picture, i.e. can't see the forest through the trees. It must be really difficult when your eating disorder tries to make you follow all sorts of rules about not eating. But if you don't eat you won't be strong enough to do all sorts of things – for instance, you told me you'd like to work as a...'*

2 *Planning – A written plan for change*

Develop a clear plan for change by writing down the headings and decisions in Table 12.3 on a piece of paper. Any eating disorder rules and/or safety behaviours that Edi discloses and wishes to challenge can also be documented.

It is helpful if these plans can set down ideas about all Edi's individual 'hot' areas relating to food, such as meals, shopping and preparing food. The structure aims to 'walk through' each scenario in detail. Talk about the changes, what needs to happen to implement them, what help will be needed, who may be able to help and then write them down.

TABLE 12.3 Change plan for eating

The changes I want to make in regard to my nutritional health are:	
The most important reasons why I want to make these changes are:	
The steps I plan to take towards changing are:	
The ways other people can help me are:	Person: Possible ways to help:
I will know that my plan is working if:	
Some things that could interfere with my plans are:	

Emphasise to Edi again that:

> *'All living creatures need fuel to continue living, therefore all human beings must eat. Eating is not a choice; we have to eat to live.'*

It is vital to *review* and *reflect* with Edi. The written plan for change can be checked later – *outside mealtimes* – for achievements and progress or problems, discussion of what went wrong and why, what has been learnt and possible adjustments for the future. After the implementation of significant changes, try to work through the following bullet points with Edi:

- what I observed when I decided to change

- what I can learn and reflect on about my change experiment

- what I plan to do next time.

Eating information

The goal is to reverse weight loss by gradually increasing the amount in the diet. This is best done by small meals/snacks regularly spread throughout the day.

- In the first phase (3–7 days) of managing people who fall into the high-risk zone of anorexia nervosa, the advice is to aim for a soft diet, e.g. low roughage, invalid-type diet of approximately 30–40 kcal/kg/day spaced in small portions throughout the day. The total will be about 1000 kcal. In some cases, liquid food supplements may be easier to tolerate than normal food.

- The final goal is to aim for a normal diet (approximately 2000–2500 kcal or more depending on an individual's size, activity level, metabolic rate, climate, etc.), with supplements to rectify the weight loss. Approximately an extra 500 kcal a day is needed to gain a kilogram in a week (but this depends on Body Mass Index and exercise level), i.e. 2500–3000 kcal per day is needed to restore lost weight. The diet on inpatient units contains about 3000–3500 kcal.

- Professionals in the eating disorder field aim for sufferers to increase their weight by 0.5 kg/week, on average, when supervised on an outpatient basis and 1 kg/week, on average, when under the care of a specialised hospital unit. A general directional trend in weight gain is, however, more important than the minutiae of weekly results.

- To eat the kind of calories required to restore weight loss in a sustained and fairly consistent way is, much to the surprise of most carers, a tall order. The sufferer may require encouragement and/or supervision to limit their activity levels to avoid excess 'energy expenditure'.

- To sustain weight gain, sufferers will routinely have to eat three meals (including two desserts) and three snacks a day (dependent on age, sex and BMI). Psychologically, and physically, it is more comfortable for Edi to have food spaced throughout the day. A consistent and disciplined schedule is therefore needed.

- It would be unrealistic to expect a sufferer embarking on a new eating plan, and immensely cautious of change, to radically alter their eating (pattern, portion size, food types, etc.) initially. A regular plan (such as three meals and three snacks) needs to be built up gradually, over a period of weeks, maybe initially introducing Edi to 'half portions' of snacks and smaller, but regularly spaced, meals.

- Some people prefer to have the extra nutrition as a supplement to a normal diet eaten with the rest of the family. This supplement can be dropped when normal weight is regained – providing reassurance for Edi. The extra nutrition may be taken as prescribed extras such as Caloreen, Fortisip, EnsurePlus, etc. or the sort of nutritional supplements that athletes take. Another option is to add in milkshakes, yogurt-based smoothies, milky drinks – for example, Horlicks, etc. Some sufferers prefer the former, being more acceptable to them as a form of medical treatment.

- A multi-vitamin/multi-mineral preparation in the normal adult dose (e.g. Sanatogen Gold [non-NHS], Forceval 1–2 or Seravit capsules) is also recommended. The children's preparations are easier to take as the tablets are smaller.

- Avoid Edi consuming and 'filling up' on large quantities of fruit and vegetables. Some sufferers may have got into the routine of living on just such a diet, which will need to be 'weaned down' gradually. During the weight-gaining phase, fruit and vegetables account for an almost insignificant proportion of total calorific intake and their inclusion is to accustom Edi to a healthy and balanced diet. Therefore, fruit (including bananas) should be considered as 'an extra' and not equivalent to a snack or dessert. Such rules should be outlined clearly to Edi to avoid misunderstandings. Maybe suggest to Edi that she or he may eat no more than one piece of fruit a day in the weight-gaining phase (this could be in addition to two portions of vegetables with lunch, two portions of vegetables with dinner and maybe some fruit content to certain puddings – fruit salad and ice cream or apple crumble and custard, for example).

- Additionally, avoid Edi consuming excessive volumes of fluids to 'fill up' or to make post-meal vomiting 'easier'. Encourage Edi to drink no more than two or three tumblers (200 ml) of water with a meal and one with a snack. Fizzy drinks should preferably be excluded and caffeine should only be drunk in moderation.

- Don't get bullied into providing fat-free or 'light' or low-calorie foods. Some oils are essential for health. Oily fish and nuts and seeds provide essential fatty acids for growth and recovery.

- It is sometimes useful to start the process of refeeding with foods that are not terrifying in terms of large or unknown calorie loads. Using snacks between meals which are labelled with nutritional information can allay some of Edi's fear. The goal would be gradually to reduce the need for such tight, restrictive rules.

- To increase weight at a maximum (but psychologically manageable) rate, the following is a daily plan taken from a typical hospital eating disorders unit. Of course, variations are also suitable and the basic structure can be adapted to suit Edi's needs. The quantity served and the regularity of meals and snacks may have to be built up over a period of weeks:

  Breakfast – 30–40 g of cereal (cornflakes, branflakes, muesli or two Weetabix) with 200 ml milk (semi-skimmed or full) *and* two slices of medium toast with two margarines/butters (hotel/restaurant-size pre-packaged portions) and two jams/marmalades/honey (again hotel-size portions) *or* two slices of toast with peanut butter.

  Morning snack/snack 1 – all approximately 200 calories. Examples include: a cereal/cake bar (various kinds), a scone/teacake/toast with butter and jam, oatcakes or other biscuits (usually 3–4), a full-fat yogurt, a smoothie, rice pudding, milky drink (latte/Horlicks, etc.), packet of mixed fruit and nuts, etc.

Lunch – a sandwich (two slices of thick bread, butter or mayonnaise), with protein filling (tuna mayo, egg mayo, cheese, ham, chicken, etc. and salad) *or* a piece of protein (chicken breast, half a can of oiled tuna, one mackerel fillet, two slices of thick ham, etc.) and a serving of carbohydrate (approximately four tablespoons or two large serving/slotted spoons) of rice, couscous or pasta or four new potatoes or one equivalently sized jacket potato or portion of bread. The protein and carbohydrate are to be served with two portions of vegetables. If you picture a dinner plate, try to imagine a portion of protein filling a quarter of the area and a portion of carbohydrate filling a quarter of the area. The remaining space on the plate is for the vegetable portions.

Dessert – a smoothie, milkshake, a serving of crumble and custard, fruit salad and ice cream, a slice of sponge cake, etc.

Afternoon snack/snack 2 – same as options for morning snack.

Dinner – same as options for lunch.

Dessert – same as options for lunch.

Evening snack/snack 3 – same as options for morning snack.

- It is helpful to have the food for the day planned beforehand in order to remove uncertainty and decision making at times of high stress. Maybe a weekly menu plan could be drawn up and agreed together. It may be important to have a rule that after a menu for the week has been written, agreed together and stuck up (for example, in the kitchen), then *no* alterations are to be made by either Edi *or* yourself.

- Keep records of achievements in meals and weekly menus/meal plans; this can be brought to review meetings.

The only way to judge whether a plan is adequate is to track the effect that it is having on nutritional risk. (Remember – weights can be deceptive so medical expertise to measure function is helpful.)

The final goal is to share meals in a social fashion and for eating to take its place as a way of connecting with others. However, depending on the individual, it may be necessary to work towards this goal in small stages – perhaps you could start off by taking a snack familiar to Edi with you to a café and sharing a coffee together. Then, maybe next time, you could encourage Edi to choose a new snack from a shop when you're out or even one from the café itself.

It is also helpful to plan to eat meals in different places and at different times in order to coach Edi to become more flexible with his or her plans. Maybe initially, choosing a sandwich and a dessert (e.g. something standard like a yogurt or a smoothie) from a supermarket and having a picnic out may be enough for Edi to cope with.

Planning meals out before the event may alleviate some of the associated anxiety Edi experiences – look on the internet together for sample menus or visit the restaurant itself with Edi beforehand just to browse through the menu board outside. However, try to avoid using menus with caloric content posted as the eating disorder almost always trumps Edi's personal preferences. You could even help him or her make a decision about what to order. With so many chain restaurants in larger towns and cities now, Edi may eventually develop a handful of 'safe' eateries – the menus will be standard between locations and she or he will become familiar with what feels comfortable for them. Also, it is worth remembering that if Edi finds one ingredient in a dish too daunting to cope with on the first visit to a new restaurant, reassure him or her that it is perfectly normal and acceptable to ask the chef to omit the item.

ACTION POINT

You may want to find out more about nutrition and refeeding. There are NICE guidelines specifically on nutrition in addition to the eating disorder guidelines:

- Nutritional guidance for adults (2006): www.nice.org.uk

The British Nutrition Foundation (www.nutrition.org.uk) has information on a healthy balanced diet and the benefits of food groups.

 REFLECTION POINTS

1. The earlier rule-bound eating behaviours are addressed with discussion and calm, consistent encouragement to motivate towards implementing healthy eating plans, the more likely the eating disorder is to follow a shorter course.

2. After every step/new change Edi makes, the following reflections are pertinent to discuss together:

- what I observed when I undertook change

- what I can learn and reflect on about my change experiment

- what I plan to do next time.

E Supported eating

If there are no signs that Edi can ensure his or her nutritional safety, it will be necessary to implement some degree of supported eating. The following account is a suggestion and provides ideas for how a home carer could set about this. Ideally, this would be a decision made jointly with Edi in order to avert more restrictive means to safeguard health, such as inpatient treatment or sectioning under the Mental Health Act.

It may be helpful to stress that, as in many other illnesses, it is sometimes necessary to take unpleasant medicine. *Food should be conceptualised as 'medicine' to help Edi recover.* In order to recover health, Edi may feel that some of the food (medicine) has unwelcome side effects or is difficult to take. It takes personal effort and strength to overcome reluctance.

Skill set for supported eating

Outlined here are the main skills needed for supportive eating. These are the essential items to coach Edi in how to modify rule-driven eating:

1. **Plan the meals beforehand**. If possible, spend time visualising what will occur (construct a 'story board'). Then during the meal coaching phrases may be used such as:

    - *'We went through this plan yesterday.'*

    - *'We agreed that we would not change anything during meals.'*

    - *'Remember, we discuss meal plans and goals outside mealtimes.'*

    - *'We agreed that our next meeting for discussing meal plans and goals is at…'*

    - *'You can write down what you want to say after this meal and bring your notes to the meeting.'*

2. **Set appropriate goals**. You may need to start with a shared snack and build up.

3. **Attainable success**. Nothing is more motivating than success, so *remember to start with goals that are attainable*. On the other hand, do not set too easy a goal as you will not get a sense of success – discussion and detailed planning are the keys.

   During your discussions, try to prepare beforehand for what may be a difficult topic, work out what you want to say and use your own words to gently point out that if there is a failure to work towards goals or weight gain, then admission to hospital or restricted activities may be needed to safeguard health. The goal should be that Edi starts to try a planned activity – *beginning and having a go is more important than finishing*. Remember the old saying, 'If at first you don't succeed, try, try, try again.'

4. **Set firm limits and boundaries** (ideally agreed beforehand) and instigate them calmly. Restate these whenever necessary, calmly and consistently. For example:

   - *'We agreed this at our discussion meeting. We can discuss this again later, but not now.'*

   For instance, there might be the expectation of *x* kg weight gain per week.

   - *'You really need to eat the meal.'*
   - *'I am going to sit here and help.'*
   - *'Afterwards we can go somewhere else and talk about why it is so difficult but right now let's just focus on eating.'*
   - *'We are not sticking to plan. Let us see how near the plan we can stay, and discuss it later.'*

5. **Remember – with anorexia, it is as if an 'anorexic minx' is sitting on the chair with Edi, whispering critical and**

judgemental remarks – *'You do not deserve to eat, you stupid, fat bitch'* and *'Who are you to think that you are entitled to food?'* and *'You're breaking my rules for eating this'*. You can counteract the 'anorexic minx' thoughts by showing warmth and love and refraining from expressing criticism and frustration.

The sort of things you might want to do or say include:

- *'Remember it is normal to eat and your body needs it. Everyone requires food as fuel.'*

- *'When you don't eat your metabolism slows down.'*

- *'Food isn't the real problem, it's feelings.'*

- *'Let's not let the eating disorder win.'*

Whatever the individual eating disorder – whether Edi is affected by anorexia or bulimia or another eating disorder – try to work out comments about how the particular minx is trying to undermine Edi's efforts to return to healthy eating.

Comforting gestures – a stroke, a hand-hold, a pat on the shoulder, distraction by general talk in a relaxing atmosphere – are all helpful.

6. **Remember to give support and praise whenever possible**, without sounding patronising by merely saying 'good' or 'well done' as this can seem dismissive. Acknowledge the struggle that has taken place. For example:

- *'I believe in you – I know you can do this.'*

- *'You are doing so well in your struggle.'*

- *'I am impressed that you have shown so much courage in overcoming your eating disorder's thoughts.'*

- *'You have been brave to stick to plan.'*

- *'I am impressed with your toughness in sticking to plan.'*

- *'You are such a strong person – I have so much admiration for you.'*

- *'It is great that you have been able to be flexible enough to change your rules so that you can care for your health.'*

7. **Help by breaking the task into small sub-tasks**. For example:

   - *'We had decided on half an hour for this meal. How about finishing a quarter of the plate in five minutes? Do you want me to let you know when you have one minute of the five left?'*

8. **Do not enter into disagreements at mealtimes** (if necessary agree to put it on the agenda for the next meeting outside mealtimes). Remain *calm, consistent* and *kind* – no matter how hard it is for carers to watch or try to help, beating the negative and persistent 'eating disorder minx' is akin to fighting a war for Edi.

9. **Sidestep any battles by calling on higher authority**. For example:

   - *'The hospital/NHS Guidelines state that I should not enter into long discussions about food with you.'*

   - *'You are free to choose whether or not you decide to stick to this plan. Remember though, there is a bottom line in terms of your health and what you want to do with your future life.'*

   - *'If you choose not to eat now then it may be that many more freedoms will disappear with hospital care.'*

   - *'My nutritional requirements are different to yours. Nutritional requirements are based on age, weight and sex. In this house, we do not make comparisons about what others eat.'*

10. **Give yourself enough time to allow you to be calm during the meal/snack**: try to make sure that meals are not interrupted by distractions, the phone, visitors, etc. Recruit others to help you do this task. Do not be afraid to delegate meals or other tasks to others.

11. **Do not give in to an automatic emotional response** when you feel angry or frustrated.

    Anxiety and anger are contagious – if you are anxious it will ratchet up Edi's anxiety. Count to ten or take five deep breaths. Imagine yourself as a fly on the wall watching what is going on. Gentle background music may help create and sustain a more peaceful mood. Ask Edi if they have further suggestions for introducing a calming atmosphere.

12. **If you see negative behaviours then state what you see calmly and in first and third person**; give feedback about cheating or rituals with sensitivity and care to avoid making the person feel shame, humiliation and embarrassment. For example:

    - *'I can see that you are smearing the butter around the plate. I would like to see you try to overcome that eating disorder behaviour.'*

    - *'I can see that you seem to be struggling. Is there anything I can do to help?'*

    - *'I can see some custard left in your bowl. I would like you to battle against your eating disorder's thoughts and scrape the last few spoonfuls out, please. It is important that we get into good eating habits.'*

13. **Set goals to ensure that you target both the eating and the safety behaviours**. For example:

    - *'We agreed that you would spend 30 minutes with me listening to the CD after the meal and then would not visit the bathroom for a minimum of another hour.'*

14. **Ensure that you notice and reflect back on the positive things that you see**. If possible, ignore the negative aspects as much as possible. Remember to affirm the process and the challenge of eating by naming specific details, rather than just saying 'Good girl' or something similar when the meal is over, which can sound patronising. For example:

    - *'I am impressed with how you've coped. You were able to get back on track after we found there were none of your yogurts in the fridge.'*

    - *'Well done. You managed to catch up time after eating your tuna slowly by eating your pasta at a better pace. That's a good improvement.'*

15. **Avoid stepping into safety behavioural loops**: do not give reassurance; control the impulse to take the easy option for the sake of peace.

16. **Have a feedback session later** (but not in the period just after a meal), where you discuss what worked and what did not work and make new plans.

It is very important to ensure that communication at mealtimes is positive and warm. Try to suppress any critical and hostile comments. This is very difficult – seeing someone playing and toying with food and taking a long time is very irritating and frustrating. It takes the patience of a saint to do this day in, day out, and meal after meal. Maybe there can be a rota of other people to help? Maybe one person in the family is particularly good in this role? (Fathers can often be good at this task as food may not have as much meaning for them.)

TABLE 12.4 Things to avoid and things to say

Things to try not to say – think of your tone of voice	Things to say calmly
Why haven't you eaten it all?	*You told me you would eat it. Please do it – I know you can.*
Surely you can eat that last bit?	*I know you need support and I know you can do it.*
Come on, you have not finished that bit, time is running out and I've got things to do, get on with it.	*It is hard but you have the courage within you to do it.*
What a waste!	*Try hard not to listen to the anorexic minx.*
I have spent hours getting that ready!	*We need to take steps to improve your nutritional safety.*
Think about the children in Africa!	*I am not going to get into a debate now. Let's get on with the nutritional treatment.*
It's disgusting to see you cut up your food like that!	*In the plan we agreed, we said that dinner would last less than 45 minutes. You have 15 minutes left. Can I help? Should I heat it up again?*
Look at how little you have taken! What do you think you are, a mouse?	*That portion size is not big enough. Please can you try again?*

F Halfway support

As well as directly talking face-to-face, there are many other less intrusive ways to give support. Time, confidence and progress will present new challenges for Edi. As Edi continues into recovery, your role will need to alter. Just think of the Dolphin metaphor: swimming ahead, leading the way and guiding the passage when Edi is helpless; swimming alongside, coaching and giving encouragement, when Edi needs a prop; but quietly swimming behind, ever present and close at hand, when Edi is making positive progress and gaining independence.

The following are some real examples:

Julie had a BMI of 16 kg/m² and was doing some temporary office work during the year off from university because of ill health. She made a plan with her father about what she would eat away from home at the office, and when. They agreed that her father would text her to remind her to eat. Thus at 10.30 a.m., the agreed snack time, her Dad would text her, 'Thinking of you'. Julie would then text back, 'Done'. In this way they were able to increase gradually the number of goals set in their plan.

When I was eating lunch or a snack on my own, I found that the 'flashcard' I kept in my purse sometimes helped me get through. On one side of the card, I had written five reasons why I had to eat (both long-term and short-term goals), and, on the other side, both my parents had written words of encouragement. The card was invaluable to me when I lost sight of the future, bringing me back to the reality of how my eating disorder was destroying me. (AC)

Meanwhile, other sufferers have found talking on the telephone to a sibling, friend or parent, whilst eating alone, a good distraction tool. Or, sometimes, if Edi (or yourself) anticipates a meal or a snack will present a particular challenge (maybe due to the day's events or the timing of eating), writing a few words on a piece of paper and attaching it to the food, before you send Edi off out for the day, may help. For example, *'This is your ticket to freedom and a future'* or *'You are so special to all of us – please look after yourself'*.

Samantha lived with her parents and grandparents. When Sam's parents reviewed progress they came to the conclusion that it was not helpful if the entire table joined in instructing her to eat. They decided that one person would be responsible for coaching, using a variety of statements such as: 'Why don't you divide the plate up into four, and plan to eat a quarter in six minutes? Then go on to the next one. I will remind you of the time' and 'You have done well, and come within that goal. Now let's start on the next one.' The 'eating coach' would sit next to Sam and quietly guide her, not including others at the table in the conversation. The other adults would try to have a normal conversation, if possible, including Sam in plans for non-eating-disorder activities.

This comment was made by another carer about how they overcome procrastination:

'She talks and talks and talks and so eats so slowly. When she's got herself onto a topic, she won't stop and so eventually we have to say, "Okay, sorry, you'd better stop talking love. Dad and I are going to talk while you eat, okay, because otherwise we are going to be here in an hour's time."'

You may want to coach a more flexible way of thinking.

'Let's roll a dice to see what extra nutrition we should add to your food today. Let's think of a different snack for each of the six numbers.'

'Let's learn how to adapt to life less rigidly. I will put different names of snacks into these envelopes and you can choose them at random.'

REFLECTION POINTS

1. Starvation is a trap. Starvation prevents the development of brain capacity to make change. Starvation removes the capacity to make wise decisions.

managing undereating

2. *Where* is the meal to take place?

3. *When* is the meal to take place?

4. *Who* is to be the 'meal coach' at which meal?

5. Skills needed by the 'meal coach' are calmness, compassion, consistence, patience and firmness.

6. Balancing the need to renourish with the capability of contemplating change is a tough challenge.

7. Society acknowledges this dilemma with the recognition that the Mental Health Act can be used to protect and safeguard the health of people with eating disorders.

8. Planning and preparation through pre- and post- discussion, reflection and analysis of what went well or wasn't so successful, is essential.

Other information

The husband of a person with an eating disorder has set up the following website, in which he describes what you can do and say to help someone in recovery. He gives good advice on mealtime management: www.anorexiacarers.co.uk.

Several podcasts about building effective communication and care now feature on the website www.grainnesmith.co.uk, with more planned for the future.

The international charity F.E.A.S.T. (Families Empowered and Supporting Treatment of Eating Disorders) supports carers by providing information and support. Parents can use the invaluable online 'Around the dinner table' forum: www.feast-ed.org.

13

How to help with bingeing and purging

Understanding what causes a bulimic mindset

Eating is essential to life. A fifth of what we eat (i.e. approximately 500 kcal) is used to power our brains. The brain therefore has a great deal invested in making sure that we eat enough to meet its needs. The brain has two main systems:

1. The 'Nutrostat' system involves 'body nutrient balance'. This monitors the levels of nutrients and the composition of body parts, adjusting appetite accordingly.

2. The 'Drive' system, which involves learning and memory, relates to wanting to eat – the desire to eat and the pleasure that results from eating and the memory of the impact of eating specific foods.

Both elements, the Nutrostat and the Drive systems, are disturbed in people with eating disorders. Prolonged starvation or irregular nutrition can cause the balance of nutrients to be off kilter. The Nutrostat system then kicks in, sending strong signals that the body needs to eat. This explains why episodes of overeating are so common in eating disorders.

The body's natural Drive system can be overridden by emotional problems, unusual eating habits and rapid changes in blood sugar. There are several factors that produce large blood sugar swings:

- Foods which are highly processed cause quick absorption of sugars and blood sugar spikes. Sugar rushes can produce addictive brain changes, in essence triggering habitual, compulsive eating behaviour, which is separate from eating simply to meet dietary needs.

- Vomiting produces large swings in blood sugar.

- A fasting/feasting eating pattern also causes peaks and troughs in blood sugar levels.

Thus unbalanced diet and eating patterns set the scene for bulimic behaviours, and extreme weight control measures, such as prolonged fasting or purging, can make it into a habit. Habits are behaviours driven by an automatic mindset rather than conscious, goal-directed thought. It is fairly common for people to engage in activities on 'auto-pilot', which allow them to accomplish more with less mental energy. However, when behaviours – like bingeing and purging – become part of an automatic mindset, they can cause harm and be difficult to shift. *The adolescent brain is particularly at risk for learning habits*, and addictive overeating can quickly become wired in. A binge/purge mindset can also be triggered by environmental conditions – for example, being home alone after work, feeling anxious or after an argument with a friend.

Reactions to overeating

You may have any number of different reactions to discovering bingeing behaviour. In some cases, when anorexia nervosa is part of the unhappy picture, if Edi starts to overeat after a period of starvation, your initial reaction may be relief because at least something is being eaten. But with or without anorexia being involved, you may feel angry at the disruption bulimia causes the rest of the family as your shopping begins to disappear. You may feel embarrassed or uncomfortable, and unsure of how to approach Edi to confront the behaviour. Regardless of your initial reaction, it is important to address overeating quickly because it can easily become a harmful habit. Vomiting, spitting or wasting food commonly trigger anger and disgust in both Edi and other people. Purging has dangers and is frightening. It is easy to want to jump to extreme measures to cope, such as locking food cupboards and the kitchen or banning bingeing in the house.

However, if strategies such as these or others are imposed, they can merely provoke cunning countermeasures and other forms of resistance.

- It is better to try to get a negotiated solution.
- It is better to have agreed rules that can be consistently applied.
- There can be choices about how to get there.

The best way to respond and to help is to use the APT strategy alongside an emotionally intelligent response:

- Try to remain calm.
- Try to be moderate, yet persistent and consistent in your response.

If you find yourself becoming emotionally aroused:

- Do some calming exercises, such as relaxation or breathe in to a count of 10 then out to a count of 10.
- Or withdraw and try again later.

Don't expect instant success. Be prepared to repeat calmly what is expected – from all members of the household as well as Edi – as often as necessary (which may be many times).

> '*I love you very much, and I don't like it when you ... (e.g. make a mess in the bathroom when you're sick to try to get rid of your meal). I still love you.*'

 Awareness

Use the assertive positive communication approach given in Chapter 8, 'Communication', to broach discussions on these issues and ask how you can support making changes.

Examples of how conversations might go:

> '*I notice that you have been bingeing every day this week, so I am concerned. The doctor says it disrupts the normal appetite control system, which makes it difficult for you to get more control over your eating. I would like you to take more care of your nutritional well-being. Do you think you could make a plan to decrease the binge-ing? I realise you are the only person who can decide to stop bingeing or not – I'd like to help in any way I can.*'

> '*I know it's not possible to change everything overnight – is there anything you think I can do to help you reduce your bingeing?*'

> '*Do you mind if I mention some of the things I have read ... suggested that it may be a good idea to ... Do you think that might work for you?*'

Use the ABC approach to understand how the binge mindset is triggered.

Antecedent: Identify what happens *before* an episode (e.g. Edi feels rejected by a friend who unexpectedly changed plans for an outing) or what factors make an episode more likely. Then think about the resulting triggered **B**ehaviour (bingeing), and the **C**onsequences, in particular the thoughts and emotions, following a binge. Suggestions of how to address and monitor the Antecedents, Behaviours and Consequences of bingeing are discussed here.

Addressing antecedents

- Minimise the food stores you hold in stock to ensure there is not free access to large quantities of food. This probably means more frequent shopping for food.

- Store foods, e.g. cereals, rice, dried fruits, in clear containers on open shelving – it will be immediately obvious when food has disappeared, which may help Edi hesitate before a binge.

- Do not have highly tempting food on display.

- Try not to lock away tempting items. This can merely increase the sense of deprivation for Edi.

- Offer to limit access to cash used to purchase food.

- Try to keep the emotional atmosphere warm by spending positive time with Edi. Suggesting shared activities during times when bingeing occurs (e.g. doing a jigsaw, tapestry, painting, sharing music or favourite TV programmes, making a photo collage) acts as a distraction but can also provide informal opportunities to talk.

- Remember that forcing or tempting Edi with food items 'forbidden' by their eating rules can trigger a binge; even the knowledge that food has been bought and is stored somewhere in the house may be enough to provide temptation for Edi.

- You could offer to talk through the situations they recognise as stressful for them, and ask what you could do to help.

Behaviour monitoring

One of the main tools to help stop harmful habits is to monitor when, how, what and where it is happening; you can use a note-book or diary for this process, though ideally it is best if Edi can do it. You could offer to help review the diary each week *if Edi agrees that such an approach would be helpful rather than being intrusive.* You could offer to model doing this, noting what happens before/after an episode

Use the ABC approach and emotional regulation to get into the carer mindset. If you notice the signs of a binge when you were out:

- Stop and pause, ground yourself with deep breathing.

- Check your own emotional reaction, your physical reaction and action tendency.

- Once you are feeling calm and collected, choose your moment to start a conversation:

> - *'I noticed signs (name the signs you noticed) that suggested you had a binge.'*
>
> - *'Would it be helpful for us to reflect on and discuss what happened?'*
>
> - *'What can I do to help you not to be tempted to binge, and to follow through by … (the behaviour you noticed)?'*

Consequences

Don't ignore the consequences for the household. Trying to avoid confrontation by covering up or cleaning up binges, constantly restocking food, etc. can result in colluding with the illness. Rules may be needed to help address consequences.

Helpful rules for ED behaviours

- You may have a rule that says that all food taken must be replaced.

- You may make it clear that you will not be pleased if food for breakfast or for a special occasion is taken.

- You may want to insist that the kitchen and bathroom are left in the state in which they were found.

- You may want to be clear that you will not supplement and support bingeing and will not give money to pay for food.

- You may want a rule about not eating in bedrooms, etc.

These rules may differ depending on individual family circumstances/stage of illness, etc., and may have to be calmly stated and restated many times.

Ideally, as stated earlier, the rules in your house will be discussed in quiet times outside mealtimes, along with the reasons for those rules, and agreed with all people living at home, rather than made in anger. You will need to think about how realistic it is to try to apply these rules and what the consequences of breaking a particular rule will be.

As much as possible, the emphasis should be placed on praising and rewarding positive behaviours when rules are kept, but with clear consequences if the rules are broken.

Try not to make sanctions which will not or cannot happen. For example: *'If you ever do this again, I'll throw you out!'*

Intense ultimatums will not work if they are imposed on Edi – it is always important to stress that it is up to Edi whether she or he wants to change. However, it is also important to stress that rules are for everyone and that Edi – as well as everyone else in the household – must demonstrate consideration and respect for others (for instance, leaving enough food for others' breakfasts, cleaning up kitchen and bathroom after bingeing activities).

how to help with bingeing and purging

Looking at the pros and cons of change

People vary as to how motivated they are to change each behaviour and there usually is some hesitation about the idea of change, as well as uncertainty, about the possibility of carrying any changes through. The 'Readiness Rulers' (Chapter 7) can be useful here, with scores helping to assess what stage of change Edi is at. Depending on the scores, Edi might be prepared to work with you on the pros and cons of giving up each behaviour. The level of motivation can vary from day to day and any positive change may take time to achieve. Take every opportunity to praise wherever possible, and to reassure Edi that you believe they can indeed make the change – a reduction of the frequency of any unwelcome behaviour is an achievement.

Try It – realistic goal setting

 Working with an agreed agenda to provide support

An effective approach to overcoming the bulimic mindset involves overriding bulimic habits and retraining healthy habits. This requires hard work, active commitment and patience as change is slow.

Here are tips about how you could provide support for habit change. As always, the APT plan is a good structure to follow.

Awareness

Monitoring or diary keeping has been found to be a key tool to overcome the bulimic mindset. There may be resistance because of shame, concern that it makes things worse, etc. It would be helpful to explore this and aim for small experimental trial periods. It may be helpful to share the positives – days without bingeing, managing to eat one biscuit and then stop, etc.

Planning

Eating and meal plans need to be structured with reminders and cues to help break automatic habits. Here are some ideas about what to include in the plans.

- The meal plan should include a mixed diet containing fibre, carbohydrates and proteins, spaced at regular intervals throughout the day. This may mean eating more frequent small meals rather than two or three bigger meals.

- Choose foods that are high in fibre and which release energy slowly (low 'glycaemic index'). These foods allow time for hormone and neural systems to activate and establish a feeling of 'fullness' and reduce the drive to binge.

- Eat protein at every meal as this helps provide a sustainable level of fullness.

- Limit or eliminate meals and snacks made entirely of highly processed foods.

- Eat socially – ideally in person or via Skype or FaceTime.

- Limit exposure to the settings, places or times that serve as reminders to Edi of overeating habits.

- Keep weight within the normal range (BMI 19–24) (Drive and Reward mechanisms are over-sensitised when people are underweight or overweight).

- Think of strategies to interrupt or delay vomiting. These could include activities that engage the pleasure system of the brain by using all the other sensory systems: for example, touch through dance or walking; sound through music, listening to podcasts or singing. Activities like meditation use multiple sensory systems at one time with slow, deep breathing whilst holding peaceful, pleasant scenes in your mind's eye.

You may need to go through this APT circle several times with a greater depth of detective work. Give praise and attention to non-food related behaviours (e.g. emptying the dishwasher, helping with housework, being supportive to a sibling) and always mention Edi's positive personal qualities (e.g. being responsible, compassionate). Keep your comments regarding food, weight and shape to a minimum. You can comment positively on the efforts made to change any behaviour, and you can comment on how hard change is.

If there is a setback, recognise the effort expended and offer to help to try again, perhaps with modified goals.

The main aim is to build towards success slowly through small manageable steps, and to consolidate that success, leading to better long-term recovery, rather than trying to change everything immediately, overnight.

Inpatient example

On the Maudsley inpatient ward, a policy of totally banning all bingeing proved an impossible task for some people, who would then leave the ward and binge secretly. The policy was changed to allow for one planned binge a day. This was included in the patient's care plan. This policy change and its discussion allowed us to help the patient to explore individual patterns of bingeing and to monitor the behaviour openly, rather than indulging in a cat-and-mouse game. Part of the contract in the care plan was for Edi to monitor thoughts and feelings during a binge. This made it possible for the nurses to help plan other strategies to manage these thoughts and feelings.

Habitual behaviour is tough to change and *any* small reduction in frequency is to be welcomed. Research has shown that it takes a very long time to unlearn behaviours, maybe up to 5000 hours of practice to change – ten weeks for each habit – in a healthy brain. With all these difficult behaviours with negative consequences, it is important that the goals set for change are realistic, not too high with failure a big possibility – e.g. *'I'll never binge ever again!'* On the other hand, if the goal is too easy it may seem to be patronising and boring. When thinking about small goals and the skills needed to achieve them, two heads are better than one.

- It is better to start modestly so that change can be reinforced by success.

- Review regularly and reset the goals according to how well things are going – be prepared to change the goals in light of experience and, if you may have contributed to an unsuccessful goal setting, apologise for the error.

- It is possible for carers, both professional and family, to work on many of the behaviours in eating disorders in the same way – by developing realistic and achievable plans and strategies for each individual situation.

how to help with bingeing and purging

14

Managing difficult behaviours

Behavioural priorities

Eating disorders are associated with many difficult symptoms and behaviours. Priority, however, must be given to the need to attain better nutritional health. For most sufferers this means eating more, or allowing the food to be absorbed by reducing vomiting and/or laxative use. Although some other behaviours – unpredictable rages, disruptive rituals or anxiety-driven disputes – may have a significant impact on others, they are not a danger to life and therefore have a lesser priority than ensuring adequate nourishment.

My daughter's eating disorder affected everyone in the house. The kitchen would be left in a mess after binges and the bathroom unusable after mealtimes. We often had to call plumbers, at great expense, to sort out blocked toilets and drainage problems. There would be unpredictable, out-of-control rages over trivia – curtains being incorrectly drawn, the 'wrong' cutlery or crockery being used, and doors being opened or closed at 'wrong' times. (GLS)

D would spend hours in the bathroom, just showering. No one else could get ready. It didn't seem to matter that my husband had to be at work on time or that my other two children needed to leave for school. It caused so many problems that, eventually, we actually moved house just to get another bathroom. (F)

When Edi is in a less dangerous place regarding nutritional risk, you can work towards negotiation for change in some other areas. We deal with these areas specifically in this chapter; first through elaboration and use of the ABC approach, introduced in Chapter 13, and then through separately tackling exemplar problem behaviours.

Ground rules

The issue of 'respect' needs to be broached as it is often lacking in the behaviour of adolescents towards their parents in general, but it particularly occurs once an eating disorder develops. Edi needs to be told *calmly and consistently*, and firmly, that a lack of respect is not acceptable. Although often inconceivable to Edi, she or he is worthy of love, support and respect, and needs to be told so. Everyone else is deserving of this same treatment and Edi must learn to treat others with the same degree of compassion, value and care they give him or her.

All family rules may need to be outlined and discussed, with the reasons for those rules, stressing that rules are worked out and agreed on to make life better for *everyone* in the household, including Edi. Perhaps some new rules need to be introduced after discussion so that everyone, including Edi, knows exactly what is expected to ensure that the household continues to function smoothly – working together as a team is a large part of collaborative caring.

Tackling the antecedents (or triggers) for behaviours

Powerful triggers for any eating disorder include *anxiety* and *stress*. Negative emotional responses to behaviours – for example, criticism, hostility and bossiness (remember Rhino?), or frequent weeping (Jellyfish?) – lead to further stress and arousal in Edi. In turn, eating disorder behaviours, through a process of positive reinforcement, become grossly entrenched.

In contrast, try to adopt and encourage an atmosphere of warmth, *calmness, consistency* and *compassion* in the house (remember Dolphin and St Bernard). By taking such an attitude, through the process of negative reinforcement, eating disorder behaviours can be extinguished. However, such an approach is a challenge – you have your own intense emotional reactions about the illness, and its impact, to deal with.

Trying to process your own emotional reaction separately, away from the general family arena, can help. At the Maudsley, parents, siblings and other carers are encouraged to have some time away from problems to facilitate this process. Many talk to others not directly involved in Edi's care (friends, carers' groups, on a helpline, and health professionals) to gain some perspective and create distance. Others find a distraction such as walking the dog, a hobby or an outside interest to be an outlet. Such time provides a rare, but very important, opportunity to reflect on your feelings and responses to Edi and his or her illness. Additionally, time out has its benefits for Edi – you have renewed energy and can continue to care consistently and effectively in stressful situations. The importance of caring for yourself was introduced in Chapter 6.

Tackling the behaviours

 REFLECTION POINT

Look at the pattern of behaviours in your family relating to the eating disorder. Could any family member's reaction be inadvertently rewarding Edi's eating disorder behaviours (Accommodating Martyr)? Or maybe eating disorder behaviours are inadvertently accepted (*enabling*) – all too easy to do. Is it possible Edi is getting most attention when she or he makes a fuss about eating, has a tantrum before a meal or vocalises negative self-ruminations? Perhaps everyone is drawn in, offering reassurance?

We do *not* suggest that you run a 'no tolerance' household or that you move for change of *all* eating disorder behaviours at *all* times – positive change takes time, sometimes quite a bit of time to work through issues and practise whatever is needed. However, it can be helpful to have an APT response. Keep a tally of such behaviours (awareness) and have times of reflection when you focus on plans for change (planning). When you review

FIGURE 14.1 Accommodating Martyrs. The family do not want to upset Edi. They are anxious and fear stoking further anxiety, or anger, and so they do what they can to follow ED rules – e.g. driving to get the 'right sort' of cereals, sitting tight in the sitting room so they do not spoil an exercise routine, letting Edi have sole use of the kitchen from 7–11 p.m. This reduces upset in the short term. Unfortunately, by following these rules they are also endorsing eating-disordered behaviour, which is detrimental to Edi's long-term health.

managing difficult behaviours

progress with Edi from time to time, this gives an opportunity to praise positive progress and discuss anything that needs more work.

You may fall into some of these traps:

- Going into the kitchen when you hear Edi starting to binge and remonstrating with them to stop *(this attention to bingeing can keep the process going)*.

- Ignoring the fact that money is stolen from your purse *(removing negative consequences)*.

- Disposing of bags of rubbish or vomit *(removing negative consequences)*.

- Cleaning up the bathroom or kitchen *(removing negative consequences)*.

- Taking the lock off the bathroom door *(encouraging Edi to adopt new secretive and devious behaviours to hide their eating disorder, giving the illness power)*.

- Giving Edi the right to sole use of the kitchen or bathroom at certain times *(removing negative consequences; making the eating disorder 'special')*.

- Accepting, without comment, that Edi runs up and down the stairs 100 times after each meal *(removing negative consequences)*.

- Accepting, without comment, that there is no food left for breakfast *(removing negative consequences)*.

- Joining in prolonged discussions about weight and shape *(giving attention to eating disorder thoughts)*.

- Falling into reassurance traps, e.g. *'No, you do not look fat. No, you will not have gained an enormous amount of weight with that. No, your stomach is not huge'* (giving attention and credence to the eating disorder thoughts)*.

In specialist treatment we have found that it is helpful to think of Edi's behaviours and thoughts being driven by two parts:

1. the eating disorder as an enemy or 'anorexic minx' with behaviours that you want to *suppress*

2. the normal part (with non-eating disorder behaviours) that you want to develop, *encourage* and allow to flourish.

It is very hard to refrain from entering into dialogue about eating disorder issues and negative self-criticism. Remember – by responding, you are validating and even encouraging Edi to think that such thoughts and beliefs are relevant and have some merit. Try to sidestep getting drawn in:

> *'Expert opinion tells me that I should not get drawn into discussing your rituals with you as it will worsen your eating disorder.'*
>
> *'It is unhelpful for both of us to discuss food. We will change the subject.'*
>
> *'I am not willing to enter into discussions about your body shape and size. You know my opinion on the issue.'*

If you think it might be useful to have some reflection time, go for the emotion behind the eating disorder symptoms.

> *'It sounds as if you are rather wound up. Do you want to talk about what has been happening?'*

Furthermore, to eliminate 'the minx', the importance of setting *clear and consistent rules* cannot be over emphasised – for example, leaving the bathroom in a mess or stealing money to fund a binge are both totally unacceptable.

Later in this chapter, we discuss in more detail how to work actively on specific safety behaviours (vomiting, over-exercising, or bingeing, self-harm and compulsions).

Rewards in the form of praise and encouragement are needed when non-eating disorder tasks are completed, or when there is an ability to step back from negativity and be flexible, looking at the 'bigger picture'. Edi needs to be aware that you recognise and acknowledge these positive aspects.

Another effective way of promoting 'healthy', non-eating-disordered thinking and behaviour is to spend quality, shared, time with Edi. Edi has your attention, and life can be glimpsed away from the eating disorder – there's freedom, enjoyment, satisfaction and achievement to be had here too. An aim may be to spend at least an hour a day together sharing an interest or engaged in an activity. It does not just have to be your responsibility. Different family members may like to offer shared walks, TV programmes, conversation, board or card games, puzzles, crafts, etc. Practices such as yoga, t'ai chi, Pilates and meditation offer skills to step back from mind traps, to forget, to relieve anxiety and to 'clear the head'. Finding a local group to join may benefit you as well as Edi.

 REFLECTION POINTS

1. Work out ways to stop any possible reinforcement of the eating disorder behaviours.

2. Try to eliminate being locked into thoughts, emotions and behaviours that pander to the eating disorder. Instead, use *calmness, warmth and flexible thinking, with no-nonsense clear expectations* (e.g. living = eating; eating disorder = impaired quality of life).

3. Try to identify any behaviours and situations that have developed at home which need to change. Remember examining and if necessary changing your own behaviours first is a good start. Look for positive strategies to help you address these. Set clear boundaries and expectations.

Working on change in eating disorder behaviours

Task 1: Using the spider diagram to structure discussion

As there are so many problem behaviours, sometimes it is difficult to get an overview of the situation. The spider diagram in Figure 14.2, illustrating some of the common symptoms in people with eating disorders, might be helpful to introduce into conversation with Edi. The diagram may enable you both to keep in mind a broader picture about Edi's health and not get focused or side-tracked into one domain.

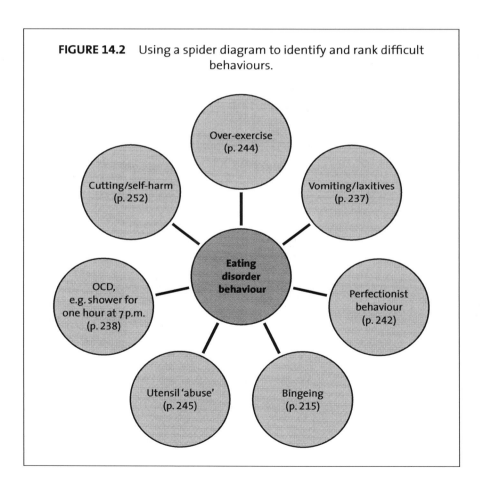

FIGURE 14.2   Using a spider diagram to identify and rank difficult behaviours.

managing difficult behaviours

Modify the diagram with blank circles, adding other symptoms or problem areas that are particularly relevant in your home and stage of Edi's illness – for example, temper tantrums, not eating socially, body checking, etc. For the purposes of this chapter, more information on tackling specific behaviours can be found on the pages indicated in each circle.

ACTION POINT

'This spider diagram illustrates some of the difficulties that people with an eating disorder face. If I were to ask which of these you would be most interested in changing, what would it be?'

Let Edi point or respond in some way and explore change in terms of Desire, Ability, Reason and Need. These **'DARN' questions** ascertain the level of readiness reached towards changing a particular behaviour and promote discussion.

'Can you tell me more about why that would be the one you would like to change first?' (Desire) or

'You've chosen "Vomiting". How do you think you could work towards reducing this? Is there anything I can do to help you towards this?' (Ability) or

'You've chosen the circle marked "Vomiting" ... Could you help me understand why you feel this is the most important one for you?' (Reason) or

'You've chosen "Vomiting" on the diagram ... Is this because of what Dr ... said about the salts in your blood and damage to your teeth?' (Need)

Check whether changing the chosen behaviour meets the **SMART** criteria:

- *Is the challenge/change **Specific?***

- *Is the challenge/change **Measurable?***

- *Is progress in changing **Achievable?***

- *Is the challenge/change **Realistic?***

- *Is the challenge/change possible in a set **Time?***

The challenge to change the behaviour should be slightly beyond Edi's comfort zone but, nevertheless, perceived as attainable.

Task 2: Using the readiness ruler to structure discussion

Once a problem behaviour has been identified by Edi, you can use the 'Readiness Ruler' (first introduced in Chapter 7) to structure a conversation in which you try to elicit *how ready* and *how confident* Edi is to change this behaviour.

ACTION POINT

A useful start may be something like, *'You have not given yourself 0 so there is part of you that wants to change. Can you tell me why you have given yourself 3 and not 0?'*

Such a conversation gives Edi the opportunity to come up with his or her own positive reasons for change. This in turn means that you can step in to give praise, so bolstering Edi's self-esteem and self-confidence to change.

> 'It must be hard in the face of your eating disorder to have come up that far from zero. What would help to take you even further up towards 6 or 8?'
>
> 'Is there anything that I can do to help you go further on the road upwards?'

You could then put your own rating down.

> 'Do you mind if I put down a mark on a parallel line to illustrate how important I think it is that you change?' (Remember to ask permission before you disclose any information or give any advice.)

This could be the basis of the start of a negotiation with some form of compromise.

If the conversation is going well you may want to spend more time on this exercise. Maybe progress to discussing all the behaviours, in turn, identified by yourself and Edi in the spider diagram. *However, if the reaction is very negative, it is often better to leave the discussion for another time.*

One obstacle to change in Edi is his or her tendency to have unrealistically high expectations in all of life's domains, so setting themselves up for failure from the start, e.g. *'I will stop vomiting and never do it again.'* Establishing *attainable* goals is vital. For Edi, a positive start combined with feelings of success and progress can be achieved if the easiest problems to change are tackled first. It is irrelevant that these behaviours may be the least important to rectify.

> '*It may be a good idea to try to change the things that would be easy to alter initially and later go on to things that are more difficult.*'
>
> '*Do you mind if I say something? The hospital/doctor suggests that it is helpful to divide things up into small manageable goals. The saying "Nothing succeeds like success" is really true – we all feel good when we succeed at something – and so it is important to set things up so that you can get this as soon as possible. What do you think?*'

When you hear a response indicating an obstructive extreme thinking style, it is helpful if you can nudge Edi into a more realistic response. One way to do this is to calmly *over-state/over-exaggerate* the response by playing 'Devil's Advocate', in which you reflect their unrealistic ambition.

> '*So you expect to succeed first time*' and '*You're saying that everything will change right away*' or '*You don't believe in "a step at a time".*'

Following these conversations, try to summarise what Edi has said.

> '*Let me see if I have got this right – you…*' or '*I think you are saying…*'

managing difficult behaviours

Language and familial traits

Extreme patterns of thinking, akin to the those mentioned here, can run in families. Also think whether any family member falls into these thinking traps, with unrealistic expectations too. Ask yourself the following questions: *Do **you** focus on detail and lose sight of the bigger picture? Do you have a tendency to be inflexible?* Talking through, with both Edi and other family members, the steps needed to counteract and overcome these extreme dispositions helps. If you feel that these tendencies may affect you, initiating change in your own thinking style and/or behaviour serves as an important model for Edi.

Additionally, watch out for any 'catastrophic' thinking; any failure or mistake seeming like a disaster. If you find that your thoughts are peppered with conditional phrases such as *should, would* or *surely*, it makes good sense to try to dampen these down. Such phrases can sound too directive, overbearing and controlling, serving actually to maintain Edi's illness.

1 Managing behaviours: Vomiting

Introducing a discussion

'I know that you want to empty your stomach after eating, perhaps because it makes you feel safe and less anxious. I worry about how this habit can damage your health and upset your appetite control system. I know that it is up to you whether you change this behaviour or not. I wondered – is there any way I can help you interrupt these behaviours? Or at least increase the length of time you can cope with the urges and not act on them?'

Strategies to help

It is always best to introduce changes relating to behaviours after discussion, negotiating rather than imposing change. To reduce vomiting, aim to decrease access to the bathroom or to prolong the time interval between eating and purging for as long as possible. Maybe...

- set and agree on time limits between eating and use of the bathroom with Edi

- avoid Edi spending time alone after a meal; suggest that Edi phones a friend or you do a joint activity

- offer post-meal anxiety relief: a backrub, a head massage or foot massage.

Negative consequences

Do not protect Edi from the consequences of vomiting. If plumbing or cleaning problems with the bathroom arise, discuss such issues, and how they affect other family members, at a meeting. Clearly and calmly ask Edi to deal with the consequences of their behaviour. Acknowledge setbacks and Edi's struggle and ask what might help him or her to win the battle against behaviours which not only damage Edi's health but also damage relationships – for example, consequences of vomiting are revolting. (Ask – how would Edi feel if another family member left the toilet, bath, basin in a disgusting state?)

2 Managing behaviours: Rituals and compulsions

Compulsive thoughts or behaviours make Edi feel safe by allaying fears and removing the feeling of underlying threat.

managing difficult behaviours

The trap

Carers often get sucked into the trap of responding to compulsive behaviour. For example, Edi may ask for reassurance that they have not made a mistake, or that they will not become fat or that they are not ugly, etc. This invites the carer to share in the same thinking pattern, i.e. to endorse the validity of these thoughts. Once reassurance is given, the anxiety decreases – this is rewarding for Edi. Thus Edi is compelled to ask the same question again to get the same 'nice' or pleasurable effect. However, the fall in anxiety is only temporary, with reassurance from others providing only short-term symptom relief – not cure. Therefore, the anxiety re-emerges and the cycle starts again. And again. The compulsive nature of the questions can be very subtle, and involves a shift in responsibility onto the carer with the following strategies:

- asking the carer if what they have done, or will do, is safe

- going over and over a decision

- refusing to do certain behaviours (e.g. eat) unless a carer is present

- lengthy discussions about food, calories, weight or shape (i.e. checking details).

The overall goal is for you *not* to get blackmailed or dragged into this 'dance'. In eating disorders, collaborating in avoidance (whether of negative thoughts or negative consequences of behaviour), compulsions and rituals is like giving an alcoholic more drink.

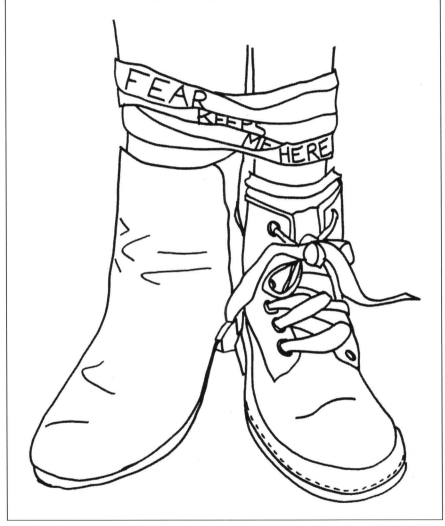

FIGURE 14.3 This image depicts how, if you start to accommodate to assuage anxiety, you can be trapped as if in a three-legged race. Fear can bind you together and trip you up. For example, if you start to provide reassurance, such as 'You don't look fat', 'I have not used any oil', etc., the rope binding you will get tighter.

managing difficult behaviours

Negotiating a plan to reduce compulsive behaviours – tips to success

- Edi should not be treated as if they are entitled to have special privileges (e.g. free sole use of the kitchen or bathroom at all times) to indulge in their compulsive behaviours. Through discussion with the family, agree on reasonable rules.

- It may be helpful to talk through with Edi the behaviour(s) found to cause most anxiety and then draw up a list of allied safety behaviour for each behaviour. Think of strategies to break/interrupt Edi's compulsions and predict how much anxiety not indulging in each safety behaviour will cause (see Table 14.1 for examples).

TABLE 14.1 Breaking safety behaviours

Breaking safety behaviours	Expected anxiety 0–100	Actual anxiety 0–100
Sit for half an hour after a meal	99	
Not check with carer what has been put in meal	95	
Not ask carer if I look fat	92	
Not ask carer if I will carry on eating and not be able to stop	85	
Reduce weighing myself to once a day	80	
Reduce the time I spend checking my body to 30 minutes per day	75	
Reduce the time I spend on exercise to 60 minutes per day	75	
Make my exercise less driven and compulsive by sharing part of it with a companion and dog	70	

- Plan for reduction of one problem behaviour at a time, rather than immediate change in every area. Trying to tackle all negative behaviours at once may lead to panic for Edi, and much less possibility of lasting progress.

- To maximise the possibility of successful change, start to target a behaviour that will lead to a moderate rather than high degree of distress. It will be a less difficult challenge and any success can be built on – and serve as a reminder that beating the eating disorder is possible and achievable by Edi.

- Some phrases that you may find to be of use:

> *'The doctor/hospital has told me that it is not helpful for me to fall into a reassurance trap with you. It only keeps your high anxiety going. I know you feel anxious now but it will settle on its own.'*
>
> *'It is not helpful to you if I allow life in the household to be put on hold because of your rigid routines. It is important for you to learn to be flexible and to be able to adjust to new circumstances. You feel anxious now but it will settle.'*
>
> *'This high anxiety you feel now will pass. What could we do to help distract all those anxious thoughts? Would you like to plan for a walk? Or finish the jigsaw? Or…?'*

- Discuss more helpful ways to reduce anxiety:
  - gentle physical exercise, e.g. yoga, dance, t'ai chi, Pilates
  - soothing music, pleasurable activities, arts and crafts
  - deep breathing, visualisation, massage, 'pampering' therapies – pedicures/manicures, etc.

3 Managing behaviours: Tackling obsessive compulsive symptoms and perfectionism

People who develop an eating disorder have often displayed compulsive traits in childhood. These may include being somewhat stubborn, inflexible, analytical, having to do things in a particular way or the 'right' way and to a very high standard. However, even if such traits were not there before, an eating disorder certainly brings them out.

The form compulsions take can vary markedly – cleanliness, personal hygiene, tidiness, ordering objects, or habits relating to food preparation, eating and meals. Some of the compulsive behaviours may appear commendable, such as a zealous application to school work, sport, dance or other leisure activity. Edi may be a high-flying academic achiever, a talented musician, a dedicated sports player and have immense career and professional ambition. Initially these compulsions may serve to reduce high levels of anxiety but they trap the individual into ever higher and exhausting standards of performance. Additionally, such beliefs serve to self-deprecate Edi further – they feel they must succeed, they must be top, they must be the best, etc. Failure to be 'perfect' is just another good reason for being undeserving and unworthy of food and self-care.

Edi lives in fear of failure, of making mistakes, of underachieving and public criticism. Edi is unable to simply accept that they have done the best job possible with the time and resources available, and that spending even more time, energy and effort may not have led to better results – for example, it is simply not possible to gain 100 per cent in each and every exam, first place in every race, or score winning goals in every match, gain the lead role in every play or be the chosen candidate from every job/ university interview. Edi fails to acknowledge that being human means making mistakes. She or he fails to recognise others have varied talents and abilities and that each and every one of us has personal strengths as well as weaknesses. Our uniqueness makes us who we are and Edi fails to realise that their family and friends love and respect them for being themselves – and not for whom they strive to become.

Edi is unable to accept their error or mistake and just say 'Oh sod it!' (Professor Bob Palmer from Leicester jokes that people with an eating disorder are missing the 'Oh sod it!' gene.)

The acronym 'SOD' can be used to illustrate how to prevent these traits being taken to unhelpful extremes:

- **S – Sufficient**

  Is this failure/mistake/negative comment, etc. *sufficiently* important to cause this much misery/anxiety/self-criticism in the long-term bigger picture? *('How much do you think it will matter to you/affect you in seven years' time and how important will it be to you in retrospect?')*

- **O – Other**

  Are *other* things more important? Do you have *other* priorities? What are they? *('Is success/praise/achievement, etc. in this more important than … your happiness, your health, your future, your family, your friends, etc.?')*

- **D – Delegate**

  Are others able to help/share responsibility in judging the importance/relevance of this error/mistake/failure? *('May I help to give you some perspective?', 'May I offer you my opinion of the situation/how I see things?')*

4 Managing behaviours: Over-exercise

Compulsive exercise is a common behaviour, reducing anxiety and producing an impression of safety for Edi.

Although exercise is usually seen as a healthy behaviour, over-driven exercise in an eating disorder has high costs. In both anorexia and bulimia, Edi's nutritional health is compromised; their body has few reserves and is 'out-of-balance'. They may have significant muscle wasting and weakness, thin bones, disrupted blood sugar levels, a 'fragile' heart and poor fluid and salt balance. By exercising, Edi may be burning valuable resources their body desperately needs as well as risking both short- and long-term wear and tear, muscle injuries and bone fractures.

Additionally, many exercise routines are solitary, isolating activities – for example, running, gym work, buying an exercise bike to install in Edi's bedroom for solitary use every evening.

If Edi's health is not severely compromised, rather than an unrealistic total ban on exercise, it may be helpful to change Edi's form of exercise into one with more of a social context – for example, joining a dance class.

It can be harmful to participate in competitive athletics when health is compromised by starvation.

By removing the solitary, competitive and driven aspect of exercise and adding reasonable boundaries and an additional source of pleasure through social connection, Edi may be able to adopt a less fanatical and obsessional view of exercise.

If Edi's nutritional safety is more of an issue, a joint discussion with compromise and a final plan – written or not – needs to be established. An example of this might be if Edi monitors the level of his or her daily exercise using a pedometer or a record of time taken, then works gradually towards reducing this compulsive behaviour. Instead of Edi running after dinner each evening for half an hour, why not suggest a joint walk for the same length of time?

When emotions have been stifled by the eating disorder, even gentle discussion of such a plan may cause fear and anxiety about change. Remember, 'One step at a time' is again the key, with no sweeping plans to change everything overnight. Patience and time are needed.

5 Managing behaviours: Intense emotions

It is common for people with eating disorders, especially when challenged or attempting recovery, to express intense emotions, even tantrums. These are not easy to manage. They can escalate to severe episodes with violent behaviour involving self-harm or damage to objects or even other people. These outbursts can happen in public and can lead to humiliating displays, impossible to manage.

> *The incident at a wedding when my daughter lost her temper, went into a screaming rage when someone made a remark she didn't like, was excruciating – awful for everyone. It caused immense disruption. I've never seen anything like it – she's an only child and we've always had a quiet house. And trying to get her home … have you ever tried to get an adult woman in a blind out-of-control rage home?* Frances, carer

Clear house rules about what behaviour is acceptable and what cannot be tolerated are needed. Previous family rules are often disregarded when an eating disorder enters the home.

Each family will have their own 'bottom lines' – rules, whether established or new, to cope with newly developed unacceptable behaviour – and these should be discussed together to ensure that they are applied consistently. For instance:

- Violence, e.g. hitting other people, breaking property, is not allowed.
- A display in public will lead to immediate return home.
- No swearing or disrespectful behaviour to family members or anyone else.
- Respect for other people's needs and property.
- If food is wasted, it has to be paid for.

The consequences, what happens if rules are broken, need to be clear and to be applied consistently, e.g. grounding, recouping pocket money, etc.

During and/or after any incident where Edi (or anyone else!) breaks the home rules, the crap sandwich can be very useful:

> *'I love you very much. I don't like it when you break things/swear/scream and shout at me – but I still love you.'*

Be prepared to repeat this message as long as you feel necessary.

Perhaps Edi cannot accept that his or her behaviour is out of line and, rather than admit it, will stamp off in a rage. Later when Edi has calmed down, quietly repeat your message – *'I love you so much. But I really don't like it, and won't accept it when you.... But I still love you. Maybe you'd like a hug?'*

Establishing and re-establishing rules, finding effective sanctions or rewarding activities, applying them consistently on a long-term basis when main carers are exhausted and family members may feel the impact of Edi's negative behaviour on their own life quality, can be a very tough job. The number of rewarding activities is limited, and possible sanctions may also be limited. For instance, in the last rule mentioned about wasted food being replaced, where this is not possible (e.g. if Edi is not working and contributing financially to the household), it will be much more difficult to apply such a rule than if Edi is earning a living.

Finding the balance between being firm and consistent about unacceptable behaviours. Modelling flexibility will also be difficult. One thing that is not possible is to ignore the effects of emotional outbursts on family life. The only effective solution is to try to tackle these by identifying ABC, and exploring how the family team may be able to help Edi towards positive change.

Identifying and tackling antecedents

Try, through discussion if possible, to find the triggers for an outburst. Frequent triggers are anger and overwhelming despair. No one has much control over outside events but one way to buffer against these emotional triggers, and to help Edi develop resilience to unexpected setbacks in everyday life, is for the family atmosphere to be as calm and warm as possible. Some tips to help you achieve this goal:

- Caregivers need to have time off. Chapter 6 explains the importance of refreshment and replenishment. Stepping out when the atmosphere is getting tense is also of value:

> *'I need to take a step out as I am getting clouded by my emotional reaction. Let's discuss it in five minutes (or an hour's) time; or tomorrow.'*

Then use that five minutes' (or hour's) respite for a short walk in the garden or with the dog; or perhaps five minutes of deep breathing in a quiet corner.

- Try to avoid getting trapped into unhelpful patterns of behaviour, such as trying to out-argue the eating disorder or depressive thoughts (remember Rhinoceros?).

- Plan your time for interventions – do not try to discuss sensitive issues, rules, goals, changes during times of stress, e.g. mealtimes, rushing out to work, when you are tired, etc.

- Notice, accept and reflect on the emotion before it escalates:

> *'It sounds as if you are upset; do you want to talk, or have a hug? Is there anything I can help with?'*

- Look for the pattern in the outburst – How? When? Why? With whom? (Sometimes Edi will identify one family member who seems to be 'a softer touch' than others.)

- Develop and practise personal statements in advance, to interrupt an incident, so that you can speak calmly when an incident starts. For example:

> *'I think we should discuss this later when we are both calm.'*

Practise repeating the statements, perhaps with a friend or family member – or even in front of a mirror – so that you have them there when needed.

- Think about how you will manage the first signs of the behaviour by trying to ground Edi into the world around him or her, i.e. by noticing and commenting on aspects of the environment. Concentrating on breathing – meditation and mindfulness techniques are useful:

> *'It looks as if a wave of anger is coming. Can you put that anger somewhere else in your body?' or 'Can you extract the anger? What does it look like – hot, burning, spiky?' or 'Maybe you can draw the anger?'*
>
> *'Try to picture yourself somewhere idyllic – describe it to me?'*
>
> *'Let's think about what we can hear and feel in the room. I'll start … there are birds singing outside and the faint rumble of an aeroplane. I can feel my feet in my shoes and my back on the sofa cushions…'*

- Comforting Edi during or after the outburst may reinforce the behaviour.

When prevention fails: Dealing with the consequent outburst

- Ensure that you are warm but consistent when handling the behaviour. For example:

> *'I love you very much but I don't like it when you…'*
>
> *'No matter how I love you, this behaviour … (name it) is not acceptable. I would not accept it from anyone else and I am not going to accept it from you.'*

- Stay calm and warn firmly, *'Please stop this, we can discuss it later'* or *'We'll discuss this when we are both calm.'*

- If Edi is unable or unwilling to listen, keep repeating your main message calmly:

> *'I love you, this behaviour (name it: shouting, screaming, hitting, etc.) is not acceptable. I still love you, I don't like the behaviour.'*

- Try to give a more acceptable alternative, and ask how you can help. For example:

> *'Please do not shout at me in public, I can see you are cross. When you are able to, I would like you to help me understand what's going on for you.'*

- Offer 'grounding', i.e. aim to shift attention from the emotion onto the environment:

> *'Put your hand on that wall/tree/stone. Give your frustration to the wall/tree/stone. Think about pouring your frustration into the wall/tree/stone, feel it flowing through your hand and fingers into the wall...'*

- Plan for a time after an incident for discussion – what led to the outburst? This may be later the same day or even the next day. Let Edi know that the behaviour was not acceptable and that it will not be ignored or condoned in any way.

- After discussion of the incident, try to end on a positive note, perhaps suggest a pleasant shared activity.

- Start to record incidents in a diary or log book for possible later round-the-table discussion with all members of your household, with a professional or self-help group.

- Do not take the outburst personally or blame yourself. Try to detach yourself from the situation and Edi's emotions.

Case study

P was 15 and had gradually escalated her food restriction so that she was not eating or drinking at the time of medical assessment. She fell into the high medical risk category and was admitted to an inpatient unit where she started to eat. Her parents were encouraged to come to the inpatient unit at times when they could have a meal with her. Trips home were planned.

However, P's parents reported that as soon as she came home P became preoccupied by her weight and shape, calling herself a *'fat lazy pig'* and making gestures as if to cut off the skin of her abdomen. P also became preoccupied about her need to burn off what she had eaten and when out with her parents would run or power walk. This quickly escalated to P having temper tantrums when she would scream, shout, swear and run off if her behaviours were restricted or forbidden.

After analysing the situation (ABC), P's parents noted that P was calmer in the morning if she started off eating breakfast with them, in a separate room, away from the other patients on the unit. She was less anxious and irritable and not so wound up and preoccupied by the behaviours and eating habits of the others. P's parents made it clear to her that hitting out in temper was not acceptable and neither was running off or swearing. They made clear rules that if this happened they would have to return P from her 'time out' at home back to the unit. They worked together to praise and encourage any control P gained over her behaviour. They thus came to take P from the unit for visits home that started before breakfast, noticing considerable improvements.

6 Managing behaviours: Self-harm

Self-harm is often used as a means of expressing intense emotion (anger, hurt, pain, emptiness, abandonment, disconnection, etc.) when these feelings cannot be vocalised or remain unheard or unlistened to. It is as if physical pain is easier to deal with than emotional pain. Following an act of self-harm, Edi feels an intense release and emotional outpouring. They may be unable to communicate their self-revulsion and pain through words; frustration leads them to the act. Some self-harm behaviours are visible, producing increased attention from others, serving only to reinforce and exaggerate them further (to Edi, a positive consequence).

As with all the behaviours discussed, an ABC analysis is useful towards developing alternative, less risky, strategies to handle the Antecedents: approaching others when feeling distressed, talking and asking for help, finding and using other strategies, such as distraction or relaxation activities, to manage anxiety.

Feedback

As a carer, you are in a prime position to give on-the-spot feedback to Edi, coaching him or her to adopt behaviours leading towards improved health and a better quality of life. Such coaching requires much patience and commitment but has the advantage of benefiting the wider family in addition to Edi.

Ideally feedback should be given immediately so that it can reinforce and encourage positive behaviours *'It's great to see you trying so hard....'*, *'Well done for....'*, *'I love it when you...'* Calmly draw attention to the eating-disordered behaviours ('safety behaviours') and give a gentle reminder – 'Remember what Dr. C said ...'

BOX 14.1 Skill set for giving feedback

- **Emphasise the positives**

  Describe your observations clearly, e.g. *'The way you managed that meal was spot on because you were able to…'* Also describe the impact of the behaviour on you, e.g. *'I was glad that you were able to discuss changes in your exercise plan last night when we sat to review things. As a result we were able to get through the post-meal phase calmly and as planned'* or *'It was great to see that you were able to … That meant that…'*

- **Emphasise your support**

  For example, *'I love you very much and I feel worried when I notice that you find it so difficult to retain enough food after a meal, to keep you safe. Is there anything else I can do to help interrupt vomiting next time?'* However, make sure that Edi understands that, although you want to help and support in any way possible, the responsibility for changing the behaviour is with Edi – not with you. *'Only you alone can do it, but you can't do it alone – I want to help in any way I can – but you're the only one who can really help yourself recover.'*

- **Balance your feedback**

  Describe the problem behaviour you have witnessed in addition to the kind of behaviour you would prefer to see, e.g. *'I love you so much. I can't accept you shouting at me/ slamming doors/screaming. I'd much rather be able to sit down and talk about what has upset you so much. I still love you, it's the behaviour I don't like and can't accept.'*

- **Don't ignore setbacks, calmly acknowledge them**

  Learn from them, plan again for future difficulties and encourage Edi to try again.

- **Stress that it is the behaviour you dislike and can't accept, not the person**

- **Give feedback in private**

  An audience is an unnecessary hindrance.

- **Involve Edi**

  Diagnosing problems, generating solutions and implementing and reviewing plans should be joint decisions.

- **Avoid criticism**

  'I don't understand. Maybe you weren't making as much effort today. You were doing so well at eating all your snacks without me being there. Why did you throw today's in the bin?'

- **Try to temper perfectionism – setbacks and accidents happen**

  Instead, focus on the bigger picture, what has been learnt and what is important.

- **Acknowledge progress**

  For example, *'You are really coping well. Two months ago, if you had ordered that same pasta dish, anxiety would have got the better of you. I'm so impressed that you kept your head. The whole family were able to enjoy a special meal out. Thank you for that.'*

  Even if no progress is being made, take notice of, and praise, any effort, as well as grit and determination.

REFLECTION POINTS

1. Changing behaviours requires an ABC approach – Antecedents, Behaviours, Consequences.

2. Clear rules and expectations are needed. Discuss these with all family members, and review and develop new ones if and when necessary.

3. Analyse ABC in different behaviours, and discuss with Edi and family members.

4. Seek, discuss and plan helpful strategies.

5. Encourage changes with *calmness* and *consistency*.

6. Have time for *compassionate* feedback where you *cherish* any effort towards positive change.

7. Review regularly and plan for the future.

8. Acknowledge setbacks as well as commenting on and encouraging all progress. Praise all positive efforts.

References and further reading

OCD

Veale, D. and Wilson, R. *Overcoming Obsessive Compulsive Disorder*. London: Robinson, 2005.

Managing Emotions

Bell, L. *Managing Intense Emotions and Overcoming Self-destructive Habits*. Hove: Brunner-Routledge, 2004.
Smith, G. *Anorexia and Bulimia in the Family*. Chichester, UK: Wiley, 2004.

Self-harm

MIND. *Understanding Self-harm*. London: MIND, 2013. www.mind.org.uk.

National Self Harm Network. 'The hurt yourself less workbook'. London: National Self Harm Network, 1998. www.nshn.co.uk.

Royal College of Psychiatrists. 'Managing deliberate self-harm in young people. CR64: A fact sheet from Royal College of Psychiatrists'. London: Royal College of Psychiatrists, 1998. www.rcpsych.ac.uk.

15

Reflect, review – and relax

In summary...

It often feels impossible to get interactions with Edi right. You may be tired, dispirited and emotional, and your reflective resources may be depleted so that you react in the heat of a moment. Alternatively Edi may be particularly tired, hungry, emotional and unreachable. However, these episodes of getting it wrong can be as useful as the ones that get it right – if you think about what has happened, what has gone wrong, and have the courage to try again. Remember that you may need to go around the APT circle many times, learning more and more each time you do it.

Also remember to take steps to protect your own health and well-being. *'Put on your own mask first'* is the instruction given on airlines in relation to parents and other caregivers travelling with children – if you're not prepared in the event of an accident, you won't be able to help or look after your children or other companions. And this is equally true when everyone in a home is affected by a major problem – in this case, everyone at home trying to support Edi in addition to trying to ensure the family as a whole will get through.

Working together: A home care team

The people involved in Edi's care may vary from a single carer struggling to cope, to a big family team of all ages and stages of life – young children, teenagers, students and people working full-time, people who have retired – all with different schedules, emotional needs and reactions to personal stress. Stress, especially over a long period of time, can affect different people in different ways. Some people have decreased energy to enjoy hobbies and other social activities, a constant feeling of exhaustion, less resilience when things go wrong, a lack of concentration/making more mistakes (which may badly affect work), less patience or increased agitation.

Family dynamics are also often impacted as people struggle to adapt to the constraints and stressors of living with Edi. All of these factors affect how home carers may cope, or not, with difficult behaviour and situations affecting everyone in the household.

Therefore, trying to build a coordinated home team to help support Edi through their illness – and to support each member to cope with individual stress reactions – is essential to the well-being and functioning of the whole team. Once the added difficulties in everyday family life are recognised, it is important to set up a 'Family Forum' to discuss incidents which are causing trouble in family life and ways to support Edi effectively. *Whatever* the home situation or 'team', a regular 'Family Forum' can provide a special space where everyone, of any age, can talk about incidents and how they feel affected by them, which may also alert individual home team members to others' reactions to new situations or incidents. Ultimately, this leads to more discussion and understanding of how that situation has affected (even been interpreted) in different ways.

Edi may protest strongly that it is her or his business – that it is Edi's own life, no one else can or should interfere. It is important for carers to stress that the illness is not only affecting Edi's health and future, it is also affecting everyone else in the household, and therefore it is indeed important for the entire family to address the situation. Whatever happens, working together in open discussion will be the most effective in tackling the 'Divide and Rule' and distorted thinking which is part of an eating disorder, and also in developing effective support in Edi's battle against it. In a specialist ward situation, regular meetings are held to pass on information and support; in a family situation the same is also needed. Without that teamwork, it is all too easy for the eating disorder to gain control; and once entrenched, without that teamwork, it is much more difficult for Edi to fight the compulsive behaviours.

Family forum – how often?

A Family Forum, involving everyone in the household plus perhaps any close others who have frequent contact, may most usefully be planned as a regular weekly get-together around a table, or perhaps sitting around the fire at a convenient relaxed time, at any time when everyone is available. The key is *regular* to ensure that everyone has the same picture of what is happening, and also to discuss all other related matters:

- how everyone feels they are coping, with everyone given the opportunity to talk of their feelings

- any extra support an individual feels is needed at a particular time

- what other things are going on in the family – exams, particular work stresses, ill health within the extended family (perhaps grandparents or others who also need extra support)

- plans for developing constructive rest and recuperation times for every family member – time to start or continue an interest, walk the dog, time out to have a massage, take part in sport, play games, listen to/share music

- cooperative plans made to enable *everyone* to have that necessary respite time – in teamwork, no one member feels alone, isolated and left to bear the greatest burden of care. While one person – often a mum – may take the role of main carer, siblings, dads, grandparents and other relations, spouses, partners and friends can all play an important part in the teamwork crucial to helping Edi

- single carers, who often feel very isolated trying to cope with a very difficult situation on their own, may find personal support through a special friend, a helpline or self-help group, or perhaps their GP may be able to offer information about a local carer support group.

More detailed suggestions on how to organise a forum meeting are given in *Families, Carers and Professionals: Building constructive conversations.*[1]

Building resilience and stamina

With eating disorders often following a protracted time span, it is important for families and other carers to recognise the need to find and develop the stamina and resilience to support calmly, consistently and with compassion over a long period of time – not easy in the face of the 'many provocations and annoyances' noted so many years ago by Venables.[2] Look for what you need – and every individual family member may need slightly or greatly different support strategies to enable continued effective caring. (A whole chapter is devoted to Coming Up for Air for carers in Gráinne Smith's book *Anorexia and Bulimia in the Family*[3]; and in her most recent non-fiction book *Surviving Family Care Giving*[4] communication is a main theme throughout.)

While an annual 'big' holiday may be the highlight of the year for many families, when an eating disorder is part of the picture, creating regular breathing spaces – half an hour to share a chat, time to have a meal away from the house, an hour or two to follow a hobby, a night or two away to catch up with sleep, or any other pursuit which gives relaxation – are often the key to survival. Longer holidays may be much more difficult to plan and organise around appointments and ongoing support.

Apart from regular Family Forums, *impromptu discussion* of daily progress/problems is also important – grab the moment of calm rational thought and consideration whenever one appears, whether in the kitchen, on the landing, in the garden, on a journey or anywhere else!

Where exchanges have been heated, allow a 'cooling off' period – after which time is set aside for discussion of the incident, what led up to it and the consequences afterwards (ABC), with a review of what is needed for the future. Try to identify any wrong assumptions, misperceptions.

Reflect on unhelpful reactions

Carers can help each other reflect on any unhelpful reactions which may be serving to maintain the eating disorder – by acting as a Kangaroo, overprotective and rushing to do what Edi could be responsible for him- or herself, and removing the achievement Edi would feel on being able to take that responsibility; or perhaps Rhino, arguing logically against Edi's eating disorder behaviour; or Ostrich, who hopes that by ignoring the problems for long enough they might vanish. And carers can then reflect on how to achieve a Dolphin and St Bernard approach to support, and guide rather than direct and take over.

Working to help with some of the underlying weaknesses

Avoidance and/or emotional outbursts and rigidity, exaggerated focus on detail, etc. are often core vulnerabilities increasing risk of developing an eating disorder. It is helpful if you notice and acknowledge any steps taken – no matter how small – to change these in the battle against the illness.

- *'I'm impressed you found the courage to tell me what you think about…'*

- *'It can't have been easy to be open about how you feel about…'*

- *'I appreciate you explaining your gut reaction to…'*

- *'It takes courage to speak from the heart…'*

- *'I'm impressed that you have been flexible/adaptable/versatile/enough to…'*

- *'You've been thoughtful and reflective and…'*

- *'You've been courageous/brave/fearless to shift from your safe rituals.'*

Useful words and phrases – which and what?

Carers will develop their own useful phrases for practising – in a mirror, with a friend or family member, to the dog – and using when needed, such as:

'I'm sorry, I was tired/cross/irritated/angry because … and I shouldn't have…'

'I was thinking about our conversation last night. I feel I made a mistake – what I should have said/what I meant was…'

Be specific – and if you can say you feel you got something wrong, it gives the message that *mistakes are OK, everyone makes mistakes*, particularly important as people with eating disorders are terrified of getting it wrong.

'I feel sad, angry, frustrated, happy about …' Carers who express their own feelings, from love to sadness to anger and

everything in between, give the strong message to Edi and other family members that it is OK to talk about, as well as show, our feelings.

All these words are powerful and effective face-to-face, but need not always be spoken directly – texting, telephone, email can also be used. A letter or card may be sent with a loving message, and be treasured.

Repetition

As eating disorders involve a lot of unpredictability with many steps forward and backwards often over a long period, be prepared to repeat what you want to say as often as necessary – *and don't give up because you feel your words have not had the desired effect the first time.* Kind, calm persistence is the key.

Letting things be

At times you will find that Edi invites you to pick a fight, or sets up the scene so that you play out the role of his or her own low self-esteem, blaming and criticising. Try to dodge and sidestep these traps – find your own words to say:

'I am curious to know more about what you…'

'Thank you for letting me know you feel I got that wrong, please can you tell me more so that I can understand?'

'I am flummoxed and confused about what to do for the best. I need to think more about it, so I want to take a break.'

'I do not want to get into a fight. I would like some time to think, so I am going for a short walk/to my own room now to do that. Let's plan to speak later. When would suit you?'

'It seems as if this is a hot topic. It needs thought. I want to understand it more. I need some time to get perspective.

> *I am going to do some writing around it to get a hold of all the issues. Let's make a plan to get back to it – when would suit you?'*

> *'I have said what I feel, you've told me what you feel; now I think we should both take a break – when would be a good time to talk about it again?'*

Be prepared to repeat, using slight variations when needed. Remember it is essential that you are calm, compassionate and respectful when you use these phrases, and remember to be aware of your non-verbal expression and your tone.

Reassurance traps

Endless conversations where you repeat reassurance are harmful. Calmly and compassionately set an agenda with Edi whereby you reduce the amount of reassurance:

> *'I understand that it is not helpful to lock you into getting reassurance from me. When you ask again, I'm going to say, "I think we've discussed that before, more than once. Can you remember what I said about the topic then?"*

> *'It is interesting that you ask me what I feel about your weight loss. I wonder what you feel about it?'*

Unacceptable behaviour

Don't ignore unacceptable behaviour. Practise your own useful phrases so that, when an unwelcome negative incident occurs, you're ready to state calmly that this behaviour is unacceptable – *and why*. With so many difficult behaviours you may need to sit back and prioritise what is most important and also what you are confident can be reasonably easy to change.

Outline the rule broken by Edi, why it was agreed in the first place and what behaviour would be better.

> 'Screaming and shouting is not acceptable. I love you very much but I can't accept screaming and shouting like that – I don't accept it from anyone else, and won't accept it from you. It is upsetting and unnecessary – if you would like the door shut, or left open for any reason, please simply say so quietly.'

VIEW

Think about possible situations when you might need VIEW (Very Important Encouraging Words), and look for positive behaviour to comment on – *'I really like it when ...'*, *'Thanks for ...'* – no matter how small the effort (helping organise laundry, taking out rubbish), let Edi, and other family members, know it has been noticed and how much it is appreciated. In so many words, express love for Edi, who may feel unloved unless it is expressed. *'I love you. I don't like the eating disorder behaviour. I still love you.'* Accentuate the positive!

Look for your own Very Important Encouraging Words and phrases, then VIEW and Re-view regularly to find what works best in your own situation.

Consciously bring attention to and stress the positive in any progress towards change. By doing this, carers offer important daily support in the motivation towards the hard work of change for the sufferer. This may at first feel a bit like learning a foreign language – it takes constant practice over time.

Other positive adjectives to use in change efforts in eating disorders

Remember that you need to notice and praise behaviours that show movement towards positive change, not just the outcome. Therefore, you need to have on the tip of your tongue a list of adjectives describing what skills are needed to do this – for example, flexible, courageous, adaptable, resourceful, brave, etc. *'I think you're really brave and resourceful to tackle this.'* Make a list (mental or written) of more positive words to add to your list of VIEW for use in your own constructive conversations.

Recording progress and setbacks

A journal or diary may be a very useful way of celebrating any progress and success, while acknowledging setbacks and frequency of particular incidents; it may also be useful in discussion with professionals. Such a journal or diary, whether kept daily, weekly or intermittently, may be individual or a collective effort.

A *collective* journal?

It is very easy to note only negative aspects in daily life. In a collective effort, with notes added by any family member outlining events, feelings and so on, with each entry – by any member – it can be helpful to develop a system deliberately to stress positives and provide encouragements by trying consciously to balance negatives with positives (no matter how small!). For instance:

> *'Thank you Edi for helping me with my homework.'*   Brother
>
> *'I felt upset when Edi argued about making tea, when we'd already agreed who was cooking and what we were planning to eat.'*   Mum

'Really enjoyed feeding the birds with you in the garden, and watching the sparrows coming and going. Aren't they funny when they squabble?!'   Dad

'Sorry I was rude, Mum, I was getting stressed thinking about eating what we agreed. I love you and really appreciate your support. Dad, it was brill when we stood and watched the baby birds starting to feed from the table with all the others. And glad I could help with your homework, little bro!!'   Edi

'I'm sorry I got it wrong when I …'   Sister

'Mum, I love walking Gem along the river with you to watch the ducks at the bridge.'   Edi

'Looking forward to visiting M with you all tomorrow.'   Mum

'Thanks for mentioning my appointment – I'd have forgotten about it.'   Dad

Conclusion

By the end of reading this book you will have learnt how important it is to be:

- *calm*

- *consistent*

- *compassionate*

- to *cherish* and *coach* your loved one with an eating disorder towards *confidence*, and

- to *care for* yourself and your whole family, by looking for practical solutions and the support needed to follow and complete the journey alongside Edi on the voyage of discovery leading to recovery.

You will recognise that conversational dances with eating disorders can be unproductive and you will have made changes so that you are *coaching* your loved one by:

- using *conversations* with enhanced listening

- *considering* your heart and head in decision making

- *clear communication, cooperation and coordination* within your family team to ensure *consistency* of approach

- *compensating* for weakness, and storing up strengths within yourself and with your social network

- having *courage* to approach new challenges *calmly*

- developing *competency* in problem solving with assertive and appreciative approaches.

With good luck and very best wishes from

Janet Treasure	Gráinne Smith	Anna Crane
(Professional)	*(Family carer)*	*(Personal experience)*

Reference list

1. Smith, G. *Families, Carers and Professionals: Building constructive conversations*. Chichester, UK: Wiley, 2007.
2. Venables, J.F. Anorexia nervosa: Study of the pathogenesis and treatment of nine cases. *Guy's Hospital Report, 80*, 213–226.
3. Smith, G. *Anorexia and Bulimia in the Family*. Chichester, UK: Wiley, 2004.
4. Smith, G. *Surviving Family Care Giving*. London: Routledge, 2014.

Index

Page numbers in *italics* denote tables, those in **bold** denote figures.

Printed in Great Britain
by Amazon

61696787R00167